The Economics of Clean Energy

Other Books in the Current Controversies Series

The Economics of Clean Energy

Kathryn Roberts, Book Editor

GREENHAVEN PUBLISHING

Published in 2019 by Greenhaven Publishing, LLC
353 3rd Avenue, Suite 255, New York, NY 10010

Copyright © 2019 by Greenhaven Publishing, LLC

First Edition

Articles in Greenhaven Publishing anthologies are often edited for length to meet page
requirements. In addition, original titles of these works are changed to clearly present
the main thesis and to explicitly indicate the author's opinion. Every effort is made to
ensure that Greenhaven Publishing accurately reflects the original intent of the authors.
Every effort has been made to trace the owners of the copyrighted material.

Cover image: anweber/Shutterstock.com

Library of Congress Cataloging-in-Publication Data

Names: Roberts, Kathryn, 1990- editor.
Title: The economics of clean energy / Kathryn Roberts, book editor.
Description: First edition. | New York : Greenhaven Publishing, 2019. |
  Series: Current controversies | Includes bibliographical references and
  index. | Audience: Grades 9-12.
Identifiers: LCCN 2018026334| ISBN 9781534503854 (library bound) | ISBN
  9781534504578 (pbk.)
Subjects: LCSH: Clean energy—Economic aspects—United States—Juvenile
  literature. | Environmental policy—Economic aspects—United
  States—Juvenile literature. | Energy policy—Environmental
  aspects—United States—Juvenile literature. | Energy
  development—Environmental aspects—United States—Juvenile literature. |
  Energy industries—Environmental aspects—United States--Juvenile
  literature.
Classification: LCC HD9502.5.C543 U6367 2019 | DDC 333.79--dc23
LC record available at https://lccn.loc.gov/2018026334

Manufactured in the United States of America

Website: http://greenhavenpublishing.com

Contents

Chapter 1: Is Clean Energy Underutilized?

Union of Concerned Scientists

In the United States, nearly 30 percent of the emissions that are believed to cause global warming come from the production of electricity, including those generated from fossil fuels like coal and natural gas. Alternately, most renewable energy sources produce little to no global warming emissions, making them a sustainable option for future energy production.

Yes: Clean Energy Is Underutilized

The White House

Produced by the White House in 2013, this blueprint details the Obama administration's efforts to place the United States on a path toward a cleaner and more secure energy future. Among other efforts, the administration was responsible for carbon pollution emissions dropping to its lowest level in nearly two decades.

Jeff Kettle

Cheap and flexible—and most notably, smaller than the width of a human hair—organic solar panels may be the answer to powering the trillions of "smart sensors" that are expected to be installed all around the world by 2020 for devices that make up the "Internet of Things."

No: Clean Energy Is Already a Common Energy Source

Larry Sherwood

According to research from 2013, there has been a rapid expansion in the development of the solar energy market in the United States, making it more than just a new source for clean energy, but a booming part of the economy as well. Lower prices of multiple clean energy components have led to increased consumer demand for the installation of clean energy generating products, including solar panels.

Chapter 4: Is It Possible for Renewables to Be Widely Used Around the World?

World Energy Council

Per the World Energy Council, the total installed capacity in hydropower development around the world has risen by nearly 40 percent from 2005 to 2015, with an average growth of 4 percent per year. The organization credits the rise to the fact that hydropower not only provides clean energy, but also water services and energy security, which leads to job production and investment in local infrastructure.

Yes: Renewables Are Widely Used Around the World, and It Is Possible for Them to Be Even More Widely Implemented

John McKenna

With wind turbines that have a combined installed capacity of 7.9 gigawatts, the state of Tamil Nadu in India is the unexpected world leader in renewable energy. Denmark, which is considered the birthplace of the modern wind energy industry, only has a wind-power capacity of 5.5 gigawatts.

Richard W. Caperton

The Center for American Progress points out that the government will undoubtedly play an important role in the United States' transition to clean energy since the federal government is and has always been a player in the energy markets. The expansion of clean energy is dependent upon significant public investment, primarily from the government.

No: There Is Still a Long Way to Go Before Renewables Are a Viable Global Energy Option

Tucker Davey

In this viewpoint, Davey points out the financial hurdles that many developing countries face with their energy needs. By and large, fossil fuels remain the cheapest, most reliable energy sources, so if a developing country wants to build a functional economy it turns to fossil fuels, no matter what the environmental costs may be.

Despite the fact that the United States government has made efforts to create a comprehensive energy policy, many of the incentives provided by the Recovery and Reinvestment Act of 2009 have expired, creating the same hurdles for investment and development that organizations faced prior to the passing of that law.

Foreword

"Controversy" is a word that has an undeniably unpleasant connotation. It carries a definite negative charge. Controversy can spoil family gatherings, spread a chill around classroom and campus discussion, inflame public discourse, open raw civic wounds, and lead to the ouster of public officials. We often feel that controversy is almost akin to bad manners, a rude and shocking eruption of that which must not be spoken or thought of in polite, tightly guarded society. To avoid controversy, to quell controversy, is often seen as a public good, a victory for etiquette, perhaps even a moral or ethical imperative.

Yet the studious, deliberate avoidance of controversy is also a whitewashing, a denial, a death threat to democracy. It is a false sterilizing and sanitizing and superficial ordering of the messy, ragged, chaotic, at times ugly processes by which a healthy democracy identifies and confronts challenges, engages in passionate debate about appropriate approaches and solutions, and arrives at something like a consensus and a broadly accepted and supported way forward. Controversy is the megaphone, the speaker's corner, the public square through which the citizenry finds and uses its voice. Controversy is the life's blood of our democracy and absolutely essential to the vibrant health of our society.

Our present age is certainly no stranger to controversy. We are consumed by fierce debates about technology, privacy, political correctness, poverty, violence, crime and policing, guns, immigration, civil and human rights, terrorism, militarism, environmental protection, and gender and racial equality. Loudly competing voices are raised every day, shouting opposing opinions, putting forth competing agendas, and summoning starkly different visions of a utopian or dystopian future. Often these voices attempt to shout the others down; there is precious little listening and considering among the cacophonous din. Yet listening and considering, too, are essential to the health of a democracy. If controversy is democracy's lusty lifeblood, respectful listening and careful thought are its higher faculties, its brain, its conscience.

Current Controversies does not shy away from or attempt to hush the loudly competing voices. It seeks to provide readers with as wide and representative as possible a range of articulate voices on any given controversy of the day, separates each one out to allow it to be heard clearly and fairly, and encourages careful listening to each of these well-crafted, thoughtfully expressed opinions, supplied by some of today's leading academics, thinkers, analysts, politicians, policy makers, economists, activists, change agents, and advocates. Only after listening to a wide range of opinions on an issue, evaluating the strengths and weaknesses of each argument, assessing how well the facts and available evidence mesh with the stated opinions and conclusions, and thoughtfully and critically examining one's own beliefs and conscience can the reader begin to arrive at his or her own conclusions and articulate his or her own stance on the spotlighted controversy.

This process is facilitated and supported in each Current Controversies volume by an introduction and chapter overviews that provide readers with the essential context they need to begin engaging with the spotlighted controversies, with the debates surrounding them, and with their own perhaps shifting or nascent opinions on them. Chapters are organized around several key questions that are answered with diverse opinions representing all points on the political spectrum. In its content, organization, and methodology, readers are encouraged to determine the authors' point of view and purpose, interrogate and analyze the various arguments and their rhetoric and structure, evaluate the arguments' strengths and weaknesses, test their claims against available facts and evidence, judge the validity of the reasoning, and bring into clearer, sharper focus the reader's own beliefs and conclusions and how they may differ from or align with those in the collection or those of classmates.

Research has shown that reading comprehension skills improve dramatically when students are provided with compelling, intriguing, and relevant "discussable" texts. The subject matter of these collections could not be more compelling, intriguing, or urgently relevant to today's students and the world they are poised to inherit. The anthologized articles also provide the basis for stimulating, lively, and passionate classroom debates. Students who are compelled to anticipate objections to their own argument and identify the flaws in those of an opponent read more carefully, think more critically, and steep themselves in relevant context, facts, and information more thoroughly. In short, using discussable text of the kind provided by every single volume in the Current Controversies series encourages close reading, facilitates reading comprehension, fosters research, strengthens critical thinking, and greatly enlivens and energizes classroom discussion and participation. The entire learning process is deepened, extended, and strengthened.

If we are to foster a knowledgeable, responsible, active, and engaged citizenry, we must provide readers with the intellectual, interpretive, and critical-thinking tools and experience necessary to make sense of the world around them and of the all-important debates and arguments that inform it. We must encourage them not to run away from or attempt to quell controversy but to embrace it in a responsible, conscientious, and thoughtful way, to sharpen and strengthen their own informed opinions by listening to and critically analyzing those of others. This series encourages respectful engagement with and analysis of current controversies and competing opinions and fosters a resulting increase in the strength and rigor of one's own opinions and stances. As such, it helps readers assume their rightful place in the public square and provides them with the skills necessary to uphold their awesome responsibility—guaranteeing the continued and future health of a vital, vibrant, and free democracy.

Introduction

> *"If we can come up with innovations
> and train young people to take
> on new jobs, and if we can switch
> to clean energy, I think we have
> the capacity to build this world
> not dependent on fossil-fuel. I
> think it will happen, and it won't
> destroy economy."*
>
> *-Kofi Annan, former Secretary
> General of the United Nations*

By definition, clean energy—also referred to as renewable energy—is energy collected from renewable sources, which are naturally replenished on an average human timescale. These sources of renewable energy include sunlight, wind, rain, tides, waves, and even geothermal heat. The most common sources of clean energy used today are sun, wind, geothermal, and biomass, which include alternative fuels like algae and methanol.

In 1975, Danish physicist Bent Sørensen posited that it is possible to live off of 100 percent renewable energy and supported his findings with multiple proposals that stand up to this day.[1] His theories were followed by further studies that showed it is possible to utilize appropriate renewable energy sources to replace the current energy system that relies heavily on fossil and nuclear fuels.

In 2017, renewable energy contributed to almost 25 percent of global energy consumption.[2] Today, fossil fuels and nuclear energy remain popular in certain economies due to the fact that they are low cost and easily accessible, especially in developing countries. Many developing countries utilize fossil fuels solely due to the fact that it eliminates one major hurdle found in forming a centralized government. With lower costs, it is easy to overlook the carbon dioxide emissions, along with emissions of mercury, nitrogen oxide, suffer dioxide, or even particulate matter in the air, water, and soil.

With human activity dumping tons of carbon dioxide into the atmosphere and global temperatures rising, continued inaction could lead to stronger weather events, food shortages, droughts and rising sea levels, and even potential extinction. Ramping up the use of renewable energy might not just bring benefits to the world's climate, it could also lead to improved overall public health, as the pollution in the air leads to medical conditions such as breathing problems, neurological damage, heart attacks, and even premature death.

By and large, clean energy sources do not have the detrimental effects found with other energy sources: they do not emit harmful chemicals into the air and trigger the rise in greenhouse gasses that lead to global warming; they don't damage land like fossil fuel extraction does; they are made from resources that renew in one human lifetime, not several like crude oil; and some even use little to no water, which helps preserve and protect the environment for future generations. Clean energy sources that do not use water mean that the water saved can be provided to nations suffering from terrible droughts, continuing the cycle of benefits from utilizing clean energy sources.

Internationally, countries like Denmark are heavily powered by wind, and as of 2015, the country's capacity stood at over 5,000 MW. That year, Denmark produced 42 percent of its electricity from wind, up from its record of 39 percent in 2014.[3] In 2016, Sweden led the charge in lowering its national carbon usage, and it has been rapidly ramping up its investment in all facets of clean energy with a goal of becoming the world's first 100 percent renewable country.[4] In 2016, the top countries making significant efforts toward clean energy investment also included Costa Rica, Nicaragua, Scotland,

Germany, Uruguay, Denmark, China, Morocco, the US, and Kenya. Many of these countries have set ambitious goals toward utilizing clean energy and making the majority of their energy production clean within the next two decades.[5]

Key roadblocks to the advancement of clean energy include climate change denial, the fossil fuel lobby, political inaction, unstable energy consumption, and outdated infrastructure, along with multiple financial constraints. In the United States, some worry that much of the clean energy advancements made in the last decade have been rapidly dismantled by the Trump administration and the President's decision to appoint Scott Pruitt to the head of the United States Environmental Protection Agency. As its head, Pruitt has rolled back many of former President Barack Obama's climate change policies at the behest of the fossil fuel lobby and other climate change skeptics with heavy financial backing. However, even among those who would be willing to make the leap to clean energy, a number of questions must first be answered about how to make it a financially viable option—or whether this is even possible—and which clean energy option is the most viable.

There are many questions surrounding the usage and implementation of clean energy in the United States and around the world. The fact-based opposing viewpoints regarding the usage of clean energy sources presented in this volume—including environmental impacts and public health problems that could potentially be caused by clean energy—offer insight into the various perspectives surrounding this complex issue. *Current Controversies: The Economics of Clean Energy* sheds light on the sources of clean energy that are currently available at all investment levels, along with which sources are truly viable for both national and international infrastructures. Additionally, this book discusses the efforts that many countries are taking to lead the way to further preserving the world for future generations.

Notes

1. "Energy and Resources," by Bent Sørensen, *Science*, Vol. 189, Issue 4199, pp. 255-260, July 25, 1975.

2. "Renewables Supply 25% of Global Power in 2017—IEA," by Veselina Petrova, Renewables Now, March 22, 2018, https://renewablesnow.com/news/renewables-supply-25-of-global-power-in-2017-iea-606070/.

3. "42%: Danish Wind Power Sets World Record Again," by Anne Vestergaard Andersen, State of Green, January 15, 2016, https://stateofgreen.com/en/profiles/state-of-green/news/42-danish-wind-power-sets-world-record-again.

4. "Follow the Leader: How 11 Countries Are Shifting to Renewable Energy," the Climate Reality Project, February 3, 2016, https://www.climaterealityproject.org/blog/follow-leader-how-11-countries-are-shifting-renewable-energy.

5. *Ibid.*

Is Clean Energy Underutilized?

The Benefits of Using Renewable Energy

Union of Concerned Scientists

The Union of Concerned Scientists develops and implements innovative and practical solutions to the planet's most pressing problems, including global warming, finding sustainable methods of food development and transport, and reducing the threat of nuclear war.

Wind turbines and solar panels are an increasingly common sight. But why? What are the benefits of renewable energies—and how do they improve our health, environment, and economy?

This page explores the many positive impacts of clean energy, including the benefits of wind, solar, geothermal, hydroelectric, and biomass.

Less Global Warming

Human activity is overloading our atmosphere with carbon dioxide and other global warming emissions. These gases act like a blanket, trapping heat. The result is a web of significant and harmful impacts, from stronger, more frequent storms, to drought, sea level rise, and extinction.

In the United States, about 29 percent of global warming emissions come from our electricity sector. Most of those emissions come from fossil fuels like coal and natural gas.[1, 2]

In contrast, most renewable energy sources produce little to no global warming emissions. Even when including "life cycle" emissions of clean energy (ie, the emissions from each stage of a technology's life—manufacturing, installation, operation, decommissioning), the global warming emissions associated with renewable energy are minimal.[3]

"Benefits of Renewable Energy Use," Union of Concerned Scientists (WWW.UCSUSA. ORG), December 20, 2017. Reprinted by permission.

The comparison becomes clear when you look at the numbers. Burning natural gas for electricity releases between 0.6 and 2 pounds of carbon dioxide equivalent per kilowatt-hour (CO_2E/kWh); coal emits between 1.4 and 3.6 pounds of CO_2E/kWh. Wind, on the other hand, is responsible for only 0.02 to 0.04 pounds of CO_2E/kWh on a life-cycle basis; solar 0.07 to 0.2; geothermal 0.1 to 0.2; and hydroelectric between 0.1 and 0.5.

Renewable electricity generation from biomass can have a wide range of global warming emissions depending on the resource and whether or not it is sustainably sourced and harvested.

Increasing the supply of renewable energy would allow us to replace carbon-intensive energy sources and significantly reduce US global warming emissions.

For example, a 2009 UCS analysis found that a 25 percent by 2025 national renewable electricity standard would lower power plant CO_2 emissions 277 million metric tons annually by 2025—the equivalent of the annual output from 70 typical (600 MW) new coal plants.[4]

In addition, a ground-breaking study by the US Department of Energy's National Renewable Energy Laboratory (NREL) explored the feasibility of generating 80 percent of the country's electricity from renewable sources by 2050. They found that renewable energy could help reduce the electricity sector's emissions by approximately *81 percent.*[5]

Improved Public Health

The air and water pollution emitted by coal and natural gas plants is linked with breathing problems, neurological damage, heart attacks, cancer, premature death, and a host of other serious problems. The pollution affects everyone: one Harvard University study estimated the life cycle costs and public health effects of coal to be an estimated $74.6 billion every year. That's equivalent to 4.36 cents per kilowatt-hour of electricity produced—about one-third of the average electricity rate for a typical US home.[6]

Most of these negative health impacts come from air and water pollution that clean energy technologies simply don't produce. Wind, solar, and hydroelectric systems generate electricity with no associated air pollution emissions. Geothermal and biomass systems emit *some* air pollutants, though total air emissions are generally much lower than those of coal- and natural gas-fired power plants.

In addition, wind and solar energy require essentially no water to operate and thus do not pollute water resources or strain supplies by competing with agriculture, drinking water, or other important water needs. In contrast, fossil fuels can have a significant impact on water resources: both coal mining and natural gas drilling can pollute sources of drinking water, and all thermal power plants, including those powered by coal, gas, and oil, withdraw and consume water for cooling.

Biomass and geothermal power plants, like coal- and natural gas-fired power plants, may require water for cooling. Hydroelectric power plants can disrupt river ecosystems both upstream and downstream from the dam. However, NREL's 80-percent-by-2050 renewable energy study, which included biomass and geothermal, found that total water consumption and withdrawal would decrease significantly in a future with high renewables.[7]

Inexhaustible Energy

Strong winds, sunny skies, abundant plant matter, heat from the earth, and fast-moving water can each provide a vast and constantly replenished supply of energy. A relatively small fraction of US electricity currently comes from these sources, but that could change: studies have repeatedly shown that renewable energy can provide a significant share of future electricity needs, even after accounting for potential constraints.[9]

In fact, a major government-sponsored study found that clean energy could contribute somewhere between three and 80 times its 2013 levels, depending on assumptions.[8] And the previously mentioned NREL study found that renewable energy could comfortably provide up to 80 percent of US electricity by 2050.

Jobs and Other Economic Benefits

Compared with fossil fuel technologies, which are typically mechanized and capital intensive, the renewable energy industry is more labor intensive. Solar panels need humans to install them; wind farms need technicians for maintenance.

This means that, on average, more jobs are created for each unit of electricity generated from renewable sources than from fossil fuels.

Renewable energy already supports thousands of jobs in the United States. In 2016, the wind energy industry directly employed over 100,000 full-time-equivalent employees in a variety of capacities, including manufacturing, project development, construction and turbine installation, operations and maintenance, transportation and logistics, and financial, legal, and consulting services.[10] More than 500 factories in the United States manufacture parts for wind turbines, and wind power project installations in 2016 alone represented $13.0 billion in investments.[11]

Other renewable energy technologies employ even more workers. In 2016, the solar industry employed more than 260,000 people, including jobs in solar installation, manufacturing, and sales, a 25% increase over 2015.[12] The hydroelectric power industry employed approximately 66,000 people in 2017[13]; the geothermal industry employed 5,800 people.[14]

Increased support for renewable energy could create even more jobs. The 2009 Union of Concerned Scientists study of a 25-percent-by-2025 renewable energy standard found that such a policy would create more than three times as many jobs (more than 200,000) as producing an equivalent amount of electricity from fossil fuels.[15]

In contrast, the entire coal industry employed 160,000 people in 2016.[26]

In addition to the jobs *directly* created in the renewable energy industry, growth in clean energy can create positive economic "ripple" effects. For example, industries in the renewable energy supply chain will benefit, and unrelated local businesses will benefit from increased household and business incomes.[16]

Local governments also benefit from clean energy, most often in the form of property and income taxes and other payments from renewable energy project owners. Owners of the land on which wind projects are built often receive lease payments ranging from $3,000 to $6,000 per megawatt of installed capacity, as well as payments for power line easements and road rights-of-way. They may also earn royalties based on the project's annual revenues. Farmers and rural landowners can generate new sources of supplemental income by producing feedstocks for biomass power facilities.

UCS analysis found that a 25-by-2025 national renewable electricity standard would stimulate $263.4 billion in new capital investment for renewable energy technologies, $13.5 billion in new landowner income from biomass production and/or wind land lease payments, and $11.5 billion in new property tax revenue for local communities.[17]

Stable Energy Prices

Renewable energy is providing affordable electricity across the country right now, and can help stabilize energy prices in the future.

Although renewable facilities require upfront investments to build, they can then operate at very low cost (for most clean energy technologies, the "fuel" is free). As a result, renewable energy prices can be very stable over time.

Moreover, the costs of renewable energy technologies have declined steadily, and are projected to drop even more. For example, the average price to install solar dropped more than 70 percent between 2010 and 2017.[20] The cost of generating electricity from wind dropped 66 percent between 2009 and 2016.[21] Costs will likely decline even further as markets mature and companies increasingly take advantage of economies of scale.

In contrast, fossil fuel prices can vary dramatically and are prone to substantial price swings. For example, there was a rapid increase in US coal prices due to rising global demand before 2008, then a rapid fall after 2008 when global demands declined.[23] Likewise, natural gas prices have fluctuated greatly since 2000.[25]

Using more renewable energy can lower the prices of and demand for natural gas and coal by increasing competition and diversifying our energy supplies. And an increased reliance on renewable energy can help protect consumers when fossil fuel prices spike.

Reliability and Resilience

Wind and solar are less prone to large-scale failure because they are distributed and modular. Distributed systems are spread out over a large geographical area, so a severe weather event in one location will not cut off power to an entire region. Modular systems are composed of numerous individual wind turbines or solar arrays. Even if some of the equipment in the system is damaged, the rest can typically continue to operate.

For example, Hurricane Sandy damaged fossil fuel-dominated electric generation and distribution systems in New York and New Jersey and left millions of people without power. In contrast, renewable energy projects in the Northeast weathered Hurricane Sandy with minimal damage or disruption.[25]

Water scarcity is another risk for non-renewable power plants. Coal, nuclear, and many natural gas plants depend on having sufficient water for cooling, which means that severe droughts and heat waves can put electricity generation at risk. Wind and solar photovoltaic systems do not require water to generate electricity and can operate reliably in conditions that may otherwise require closing a fossil fuel-powered plant.

The risk of disruptive events will also increase in the future as droughts, heat waves, more intense storms, and increasingly severe wildfires become more frequent due to global warming—increasing the need for resilient, clean technologies.

Notes

[1] Environmental Protection Agency. 2017. Inventory of US Greenhouse Gas Emissions and Sinks: 1990-2015.

[2] Energy Information Agency (EIA). 2017. How much of the US carbon dioxide emissions are associated with electricity generation?

[3] Intergovernmental Panel on Climate Change (IPCC). 2011. IPCC Special Report on Renewable Energy Sources and Climate Change Mitigation. Prepared by Working Group III of the Intergovernmental Panel on Climate Change [O. Edenhofer, R. Pichs-Madruga, Y. Sokona, K. Seyboth, P. Matschoss, S. Kadner, T. Zwickel, P. Eickemeier, G. Hansen, S. Schlömer, C. von Stechow (eds)]. Cambridge University Press, Cambridge, United Kingdom and New York, NY, USA, 1075 pp. (Chapter 9).

[4] Union of Concerned Scientists (UCS). 2009. Clean Power Green Jobs.

[5] National Renewable Energy Laboratory (NREL). 2012. Renewable Electricity Futures Study. Volume 1, pg. 210.

[6] Epstein, P.R.,J. J. Buonocore, K. Eckerle, M. Hendryx, B. M. Stout III, R. Heinberg, R. W. Clapp, B. May, N. L. Reinhart, M. M. Ahern, S. K. Doshi, and L. Glustrom. 2011. Full cost accounting for the life cycle of coal in "Ecological Economics Reviews." Ann. N.Y. Acad. Sci. 1219: 73–98.

[7] Renewable Electricity Futures Study. 2012.

[8] NREL. 2016. Estimating Renewable Energy Economic Potential in the United States: Methodology and Initial Results.

[9] Renewable Electricity Futures Study. 2012.

IPCC Special Report on Renewable Energy Sources and Climate Change Mitigation. Prepared by Working Group III of the Intergovernmental Panel on Climate Change. 2011.

UCS. 2009. Climate 2030: A national blueprint for a clean energy economy.

[10] American Wind Energy Association (AWEA). 2017. AWEA US Wind Industry Annual Market Report: Year Ending 2016. Washington, D.C.: American Wind Energy Association.

[11] Wiser, Ryan, and Mark Bolinger. 2017. 2016 Wind Technologies Market Report. US Department of Energy.

[12] The Solar Foundation. 2017. National Solar Jobs Census 2016.

[13] Navigant Consulting. 2009. Job Creation Opportunities in Hydropower.

[14] Geothermal Energy Association. 2010. Green Jobs through Geothermal Energy.

[15] UCS. 2009. Clean Power Green Jobs.

[16] Environmental Protection Agency. 2010. Assessing the Multiple Benefits of Clean Energy: A Resource for States. Chapter 5.

[17] UCS. 2009. Clean Power Green Jobs.

[18] Deyette, J., and B. Freese. 2010. Burning coal, burning cash: Ranking the states that import the most coal. Cambridge, MA: Union of Concerned Scientists.

[20] SEIA. 2017. Solar Market Insight Report 2017 Q2.

[21] AWEA. 2017. AWEA US Wind Industry Annual Market Report: Year Ending 2016. Washington, D.C.: American Wind Energy Association.

[22] UCS. 2009. Clean Power Green Jobs.

[23] UCS. 2011. A Risky Proposition: The financial hazards of new investments in coal plants.

[24] EIA. 2013. US Natural Gas Wellhead Price.

[25] Unger, David J. 2012. Are renewables stormproof? Hurricane Sandy tests solar, wind. The Christian Science Monitor. November 19.

[26] Department of Energy. 2017 US Energy and Employment Report.

Blueprint for a Clean and Secure Energy Future

The White House

The archive of the Obama-era White House website provides the permanent record of the accomplishments and missions of the Obama Administration (2009-2017). The website provides details of President Obama's accomplishments in advancing the American efforts to combat pollution and climate change.

The United States is on the path to a cleaner and more secure energy future. Since President Obama took office, responsible oil and gas production has increased each year, while oil imports have fallen to a 20 year low; renewable electricity generation from wind, solar, and geothermal sources has doubled; And our emissions of the dangerous carbon pollution that threatens our planet have fallen to their lowest level in nearly two decades. In short, the President's approach is working. It's a winning strategy for the economy, energy security, and the environment.

But even with this progress, there is more work to do. Rising gas prices serve as a reminder that we are still too reliant on oil, which comes at a cost to American families and businesses. While there's no overnight solution to address rising gas prices in the short term, President Obama today reiterated his commitment to a sustained, all-of-the-above energy strategy and urged Congress to take up common-sense proposals that will further reduce our dependence on oil, better protect consumers from spikes in gas prices, and reduce pollution.

"FACT SHEET: President Obama's Blueprint for a Clean and Secure Energy Future," The White House, March 15, 2013. https://obamawhitehouse.archives.gov/the-press-office/2013/03/15/fact-sheet-president-obama-s-blueprint-clean-and-secure-energy-future. Licensed under CC BY 3.0 United States.

Background: The Energy Security Trust

The Obama Administration is calling on Congress to establish a new Energy Security Trust, which is designed to invest in breakthrough research that will make the technologies of the future cheaper and better—technologies that will protect American families from spikes in gas prices and allow us to run our cars and trucks on electricity or homegrown fuels.

The Energy Security Trust, which builds on a proposal supported by a broad bipartisan coalition including retired military leaders, will provide a reliable stream of funding for critical, breakthrough research focused on developing cost-effective transportation alternatives.

The President's proposal sets aside $2 billion over 10 years and will support research into a range of cost-effective technologies—like advanced vehicles that run on electricity, homegrown biofuels, fuel cells, and domestically produced natural gas. The mandatory funds would be set aside from royalty revenues generated by oil and gas development in Federal waters of the Outer Continental Shelf (OCS), already included in the administration's five year plan. These revenues are projected to increase over the next several years based on a combination of leasing, production, and price trends, with additional revenues potentially generated as a result of reforms being proposed in the FY 2014 Budget. The Trust is paid for within the context of the overall budget.

Paired with other Administration policies, including our historic new fuel economy standards, the Trust would help solidify America's position as a world leader in advanced transportation technology.

For example, the Environmental Protection Agency (EPA) has released a new report that underscores the progress we have made to improve fuel economy, save American families money at the pump, and reduce carbon pollution that contributes to climate change. According to the report, from 2007 to 2012, EPA estimates that CO_2 emissions have decreased by 13 percent and fuel economy values have increased by 16 percent. In addition, compared to five years ago, consumers have twice as many hybrid and diesel vehicle choices, a growing set of plug-in electric vehicle options, and a six-fold increase in the number of car models with combined city/highway fuel economy of 30 mpg or higher.

The Energy Security Trust builds on this historic progress, continuing to increase momentum towards to a cleaner, more efficient fleet that is good for consumers, increases energy independence, and cuts carbon pollution.

Producing More American Energy

President Obama is committed to an "all-of-the-above" approach that develops all American energy sources in a safe and responsible way and builds a clean and secure energy future. That's why the President's plan:

- Challenges Americans to double renewable electricity generation again by 2020. In order to double generation from wind, solar, and geothermal sources by 2020, relative to 2012 levels, the President called on Congress to make the renewable energy Production Tax Credit permanent and refundable, which will provide incentive and certainty for investments in new clean energy. Instead of continuing century-old subsidies to oil companies, the President believes that we need to invest in the energy of the future. During the President's first term, clean energy tax incentives attracted billions of dollars in private investment in almost 50,000 clean energy projects, creating tens of thousands of jobs. Permanent extension keeps the momentum building, while creating new jobs in clean energy.
- Directs the Interior Department to make energy project permitting more robust. Last year, the President set a goal to permit 10,000 megawatts of renewables on public lands—a goal the Interior Department achieved. But there is more work to do. That is why the Department is continuing to take steps to enable responsible development of American energy on public lands. In support of this work, the President's Budget

will increase funding for energy programs of the Bureau of Land Management by roughly 20 percent. A significant share of these resources will support better permitting processes for oil and gas, renewable energy, and infrastructure, including the transition to an electronic, streamlined system for oil and gas permits that will significantly reduce the time for approval of new drilling projects. The Department will also propose more diligent development of oil and gas leases through shorter primary lease terms, stricter enforcement of lease terms, and monetary incentives to get leases into production.

- Commits to safer production and cleaner electricity from natural gas. Our domestic natural gas resources are reducing energy costs across the economy—for manufacturers investing in new facilities and families benefiting from lower heating costs. This abundant, nearly 100-year resource can support new jobs and growth, but there are steps we should take to make this growth safe and responsible. The President's budget will invest more than $40 million in research to ensure safe and responsible natural gas production. And as part of a $375 million investment in cleaner energy from fossil fuels, the President's budget includes significant funding for clean coal technology and a new $25 million prize for the first, natural gas combined cycle power plant to integrate carbon capture and storage.

- Supports a responsible nuclear waste strategy. Under President Obama's direction, the Energy Department created a Blue Ribbon Commission on America's Nuclear Future to recommend how to manage the challenges associated with nuclear waste storage and disposal. After careful consideration of the Commission's input, the Administration has issued a strategy for action in response to the recommendations and looks forward to working with Congress on implementing policies that ensure that our Nation can continue to rely on carbon-free nuclear power.

Investing in Energy Security

During the President's first term, the United States cut foreign oil imports by more than 3.6 million barrels per day, more than under any other President. To ensure that we continue on a path towards greater energy security, the President's plan:

- Sets a goal to cut net oil imports in half by the end of the decade. Increased production of domestic oil, natural gas, and biofuels, and improvements in the fuel economy of our cars and trucks allowed the United States to cut imports of oil by almost one-third since 2008. To build on this progress, the President will direct new policies and investments to set us on a course to cut net oil imports in half by the end of the decade, relative to 2008 levels.

- Commits to partnering with the private sector to adopt natural gas and other alternative fuels in the Nation's trucking fleet. Private sector investments are building natural gas fueling infrastructure across the United States just as natural gas vehicle research is making the technology more economically and environmentally effective. The President is committed to accelerating the growth of this domestically abundant fuel and other alternative fuels in the transportation sector in a way that benefits our planet, our economy, and our energy security: putting in place new incentives for medium- and heavy-duty trucks that run on natural gas or other alternative fuels, providing a credit for 50 percent of the incremental cost of a dedicated alternative-fuel truck for a five-year period; supporting research to ensure the safe and responsible use of natural gas; and funding to support a select number of deployment communities: real-world laboratories that leverage limited federal resources to develop different models to deploy advanced vehicles at scale.

Making Energy Go Farther Across the Economy

Cutting the amount of energy we waste in our cars and trucks, in our homes, buildings, and in our factories, will make us a stronger, more resilient, and more competitive economy. Improvements in energy efficiency are critical to building a clean and secure energy future. To advance this priority, the President's plan:

- Establishes a new goal to double American energy productivity by 2030. The President has set a goal to cut our economy's energy waste in half over the next twenty years. More specifically, the Administration will take action aimed at doubling the economic output per unit of energy consumed in the United States by 2030, relative to 2010 levels. This includes a new Energy Efficiency Race to the Top challenge; building on the success of existing partnerships with the public and private sectors to promote energy efficiency; and continuing investments in technologies that improve energy productivity and cut waste.
- Challenges States to Cut Energy Waste and Support Energy Efficiency and Modernize the Grid. Modeled after a successful Administration approach in education reform designed to promote forward-leaning policies at the State-level, the Budget includes $200 million in one-time funding for Race to the Top performance based awards to support State governments that implement effective policies to cut energy waste and modernize the grid. Key opportunities for States include: modernizing utility regulations to encourage cost-effective investments in efficiency like combined heat and power, clean distributed generation, and demand response resources; enhancing customer access to data; investments that improve the reliability, security and resilience of the grid; and enhancing the sharing of information regarding grid conditions.
- Commits to build on the success of existing partnerships with the public and private sector to use energy wisely. Over the next four years, the President is committed to

accelerating progress on energy productivity including through the Better Buildings Challenge, improving energy data access for consumers through the "Green Button" initiative, and making appliances even more efficient - saving consumers money, spurring innovation, and strengthening domestic manufacturing.

- Calls for sustained investments in technologies that promote maximum productivity of energy use and reduce waste. The President's Budget expands applied research and development of innovative manufacturing processes and advanced industrial materials. These innovations will enable US companies to cut manufacturing costs, enhance the productivity of their investments and workforce, and reduce the life-cycle energy consumption of technologies, while improving product quality and accelerating product development.

International Leadership

The Administration has worked not only to strengthen our energy security at home, but also around the world. In concert with our domestic actions, we have pursued a robust international agenda that:

- Leads efforts through the Clean Energy Ministerial and other fora to promote energy efficiency and the development and deployment of clean energy. Our efforts have helped to accelerate the global dissemination of energy-efficient equipment and appliances through the Super-Efficient Equipment and Appliance Deployment (SEAD) Initiative, improved energy savings in commercial building and industry through the Global Superior Energy Performance Partnership (GSEP), and supported the large-scale deployment of renewable energy through the 21st Century Power Partnership.
- Works through the G20 and other fora toward the global phase out of inefficient fossil fuel subsidies. Inefficient

subsidies exact a steep toll on our economies, our energy security, and our environment, and the United States is leading efforts internationally to accelerate progress in eliminating them.

- Promotes safe and responsible oil and natural gas development. The Administration has worked to promote safe and responsible oil and natural gas production through initiatives like the Energy Governance and Capacity Initiative, which provides technical and capacity building assistance to countries that are on the verge of becoming the world's next generation of oil and gas producers, and the Unconventional Gas Technological Engagement Program, which works to help countries with unconventional natural gas resources to identify and develop them safely and economically and can support switching from coal to cleaner-burning natural gas.
- Updates our international capabilities to strengthen energy security. We are working with the International Energy Agency (IEA) and others to ensure that our international institutions and processes reflect changes in global energy markets.
- Supports American nuclear exports. We are providing increased support for American nuclear technology and supply chains to promote safe, secure, low-carbon nuclear power growth in countries that are pursuing nuclear energy as part of their energy mix.

How Solar Energy Can Power the Internet of Things

Jeff Kettle

A lecturer in electronic engineering at Bangor University in Wales, UK, Jeff Kettle's expertise is in semiconductor device fabrication, characterization, and modeling. He has been published in international journals on over thirty occasions and is currently researching sensor development, nanofabrication, solar energy, and light emitting diodes.

It could herald a great leap forward in the way we live our lives. The internet of things, the idea that objects can be interconnected via a global network, will run your home, keep you healthy and even check how much food is in your fridge. It will mean a trillion new "smart sensors" being installed around the world by 2020. But what's going to power these devices?

In some cases, the energy source is obvious: sensors in fridges or traffic lights can simply tap into mains electricity. But it's much trickier to power something that detects water quality in remote reservoirs, cracks in railway lines, or whether a farmer's cows are happy and healthy.

Organic solar panels might be the answer. They're cheap, and are flexible enough to power minuscule sensors whatever their shape. The cells can be just two micrometres thick—around a 50th the width of a human hair—but they are able to absorb a huge amount of light for such a thin surface.

These organic photovoltaics (OPVs) differ from silicon solar cells as they can be made entirely from specially-synthesised organic materials, which are deposited onto cheap substrates such as PET, a form of polyester also used in soft drink bottles and crisp packets. This material is lighter, more flexible and can even be tuned to provide different colours—who said solar cells have to be plain black?

Critically, it takes just one day for OPVs to earn back the energy invested in their manufacture, known as the "energy payback time," which compares to around one to two years for regular silicon solar cells.

Organic photovoltaics can also be moulded onto 3-D surfaces such as roof tiling or even clothing. In our latest research, colleagues and I demonstrated that this makes them more effective at capturing diffuse or slanting light. This wouldn't make much difference for a regular solar farm in a sunny country, but cloudier places at higher latitudes would see benefits. For the internet of things, however, these improvements are a game-changer. Few of those trillion sensors will be placed conveniently in the sunshine, facing upwards; far more will be in unusual locations where light only falls indirectly. Tiny organic solar cells will enable energy to be captured throughout the day, even indoors or when attached to clothes.

From Billions to Trillions

There's no denying the huge need for such a technology. The "trillion sensors" figure at first seems outlandish, but consider the fact that a typical smartphone, for example, possesses around ten smart sensors that measure light, temperature, sound, touch, movement, position, humidity and more. More than a billion smartphones will be sold this year, so that's 10 billion new sensors just in phones. And not all smart sensors are confined to smartphones, of course; they are already routinely used in personal care, environmental monitoring, security and transport.

Whatever the exact numbers, we can assume that many, many more sensors will be deployed in future and their complexity and usefulness is growing exponentially. My colleagues and I at Bangor are interested in how we could power them all, which is what led us to organic solar.

Though engineers will always try to reduce energy consumption through better design and putting sensors to "sleep" when they are not required, even ultra-low power sensors still consume around 3.5mW (milliWatts) per measurement. Poorer quality sensors might use considerably more.

Now assuming the "average" sensor actually consumes 5mW per measurement, and assuming one measurement is made every minute and takes 30 seconds to complete, this average smart sensor will need 22 Wh (watt-hours) in a calendar year. On it's own, this is not a substantial value and equivalent to running your TV for about five minutes.

But it all adds up. Based on this simple analysis, 1 trillion sensors will use 21,900 Gigawatt hours (GWh) per year. That's an incredible demand on electricity grids, equivalent to the combined output from a few typical nuclear power plants. This is all before considering the extra demand needed by data centres to handle and store such large sums of information.

Yes, low-power electronics will be developed that should reduce the amount of energy that the sensors need. But, for long term operation, many sensors can't rely upon an internal battery, as a battery has a finite energy store. This is particularly pertinent as many smart sensors may be placed in remote locations, often far from the electricity grid or without a power connection.

Therefore we must create smart sensors that can harvest their own energy from the local environment—and it's here that organic solar technology will find its niche.

The US Solar Market Is On the Rise

Larry Sherwood

Larry Sherwood is President and CEO of the Interstate Renewable Energy Council and the author of the annual IREC Report, the US Solar Market Trends, *and serves as editor of the* IREC Small Wind Newsletter.

Solar energy markets are booming in the United States due to falling photovoltaic (PV) prices, strong consumer demand, available financing, renewable portfolio standards (RPSs), and financial incentives from the federal government, states and utilities. Thirty-four percent more PV capacity was installed in 2013 than the year before. Developers completed three large concentrating solar power (CSP) plants with a combined capacity of nearly 0.8 GW_{AC} at the end of 2013. Solar installations accounted for 31 percent of all electric power installations completed in 2013.

The federal Investment Tax Credit (ITC) of 30 percent of the installed cost is an important foundational incentive for most installations. Installed prices for distributed PV installations fell by at least 11 percent in 2013 and have fallen by 44 percent since 2009. The prices of some individual system components, especially modules, have fallen even more. Lower prices increase consumer demand for solar installations.

Important Current Trends

Photovoltaic

- California was the most important market in 2013. Fifty-seven percent of US capacity installed in 2013 occurred in the Golden State, and the capacity installed during 2013 was 161 percent greater than what was installed in 2012.

"US Solar Market Trends 2013," by Larry Sherwood, Interstate Renewable Energy Council, Inc. (IREC), July 2014. Reprinted by permission.

- Residential capacity installed in 2013 grew by 68 percent in the US, fueled by the increasing use of leases and third-party ownership of these systems. Over 145,000 residential PV systems were installed during the year.
- Utility sector capacity installed grew by 47 percent. Ten PV installations, each larger than 100 MW_{DC}, were completed in 2013.
- Hawaii had the highest per capita installed capacity of PV systems. More than 75 percent of grid-connected PV system capacity installed in 2013 was concentrated in California, Arizona and North Carolina.

Concentrating Solar Power

The most CSP capacity ever installed in the United States in a single year was in 2013. Three new CSP solar plants with a total capacity of 766 MW_{AC} were completed, the first in the US since 2010.

Over the near term, the prospect for growth in solar installations is bright in all sectors. The residential sector is growing in a large number of states, and many utility sector projects are under construction or contracted and will be completed in 2014 or later. The federal ITC, continued falling prices, state RPSs, and on-going net metering policies will sustain the market.

Introduction

The solar market, while relatively young, is an increasingly important and vital part of the American economy. What are the trends in this market, and what forces are at work? Which sectors of the market are strongest, and why? What are the prospects for solar energy in the near future?

This report answers these questions by providing public data on US solar electric installations by technology, state and market sector. Public data on solar installations help industry, government and non-profit organizations improve their efforts to increase the number (and capacity) of solar installations across the United States. Analysis of multi-year installation trends and state installation data helps these stakeholders learn more about state solar markets, and evaluate the effectiveness of marketing, financial incentives and education initiatives.

Different solar energy technologies create energy for different end uses. This report covers solar technologies that produce electricity, including photovoltaics (PV) and concentrating solar power (CSP). Other solar technologies provide hot water, space heat and space cooling, but they are not addressed in this report.

PV cells are semi-conductor devices that generate electricity when exposed to the sun. Manufacturers assemble the cells into modules, which can be installed on buildings or parking structures, or as ground-mounted arrays. Modern PV was invented in the 1950s and first used to power satellites. As prices declined, PV systems were installed in many off-grid installations, (i.e., installations not connected to the utility grid). In the last decade, grid-connected applications have become the largest sector for PV installations. PV is used in large and small installations, either on the customer or utility side of the meter.

CSP systems use mirrors and collecting receivers to heat a fluid to a high temperature (from 300°F to more than 1,000°F), and then run the heat extracted from the fluid through a traditional turbine power generator or Stirling engine. CSP can also be paired with existing or new traditional power plants, providing high-temperature heat into the thermal cycle. These generating stations typically produce bulk power on the utility side of the meter rather than generating electricity on the customer side of the meter. CSP plants were first installed in the United States in the early 1980s, with installations continuing through the early 1990s. Most of these installations still generate power today. Until recently, few new systems had been installed since the early 1990s. Installations have resumed, with three large plants completed in 2013 and additional plants under construction for completion in future years. In another application, concentrating solar thermal can provide high-temperature solar process heat for industrial or commercial applications. A few such systems are installed each year. Concentrating PV systems are classified in this report as PV installations and not as CSP installations.

With respect to PV, the United States is only a small, but growing, part of a robust global solar market. China and Japan had the largest growth of any country in 2013, and are now the largest markets for PV. With this development, the largest markets moved out of Europe for the first time in many years. US installations accounted for about 12 percent of the global total in 2013 and ranked third globally. Germany and other European markets had been the largest global markets for many years. However, in Germany, less PV capacity was installed in 2013 than in 2012.

This report compares market trends on the basis of capacity installed and number of installations.

- Annual capacity installed or the capacity installed in a specific year refers to the capacity in megawatts (MW) or gigawatts (GW) installed in that specific year.
- Cumulative capacity installed refers to the capacity of installations in all years through 2013.
- When the report discusses the annual number of installations, it means the number of separate installations of any size completed that year.
- The cumulative number of installations means the total number of all the installations that have been built, irrespective of size, in all years.

Total Solar Installations

In 2013, solar installations (including both PV and CSP) accounted for 31 percent of new electricity generation installed during the year. In 2012, PV installations accounted for 12 percent of new additions. The electricity generated by PV and CSP installations supplied 0.4 percent of all electricity generation in the US during 2013.

Recently, electricity consumption in the nation has been relatively flat. Overall electricity consumption grew by only

0.2 percent in 2013 (compared with 2012) and was two percent less than total electricity consumption in 2010. The low growth is partly due to the weaker economy in recent years and partly due to energy efficiency improvements.

Thus, additions to the grid are not supplying electricity growth, but are instead offset by reductions in the electricity currently supplied to the grid, such as the retirement of older power plants or the reduced use of existing power plants. This presents a conflict, which is increasingly apparent, between utilities and solar proponents. When the total capacity of solar installations was much smaller, the new capacity was easily absorbed. Now, as PV installations are becoming larger and more numerous, decisions must be made about how to integrate this capacity into the grid. Not surprisingly, the affected parties have differing opinions on how to do this. Low growth in electricity sales intensifies this conflict. Regional differences and the high concentration of solar installations in a few states demonstrate the varying impact in different parts of the country.

Photovoltaics

Overall Trends in Installations and Capacity
2013 was another banner year for PV, with large increases in both the number and capacity of facilities. The capacity of 2013 PV installations increased by 34 percent to 4.6 GW_{DC} compared with 2012. However, while the annual capacity growth rate was strong, it was the lowest rate since 2006. The compound annual growth rate for the last 10 years is an astounding 55 percent. In 2013, the capacity installed of utility installations increased by 48 percent compared with 2012, and distributed installations, largely on residential, commercial and government buildings, increased by 17 percent. The residential portion of distributed capacity increased by 68 percent in 2013. California led national growth with a 161 percent increase in capacity installed in 2013 (compared with 2012). In fact, without California, the installation trends were not positive –

18 percent less PV capacity was installed outside California in 2013 compared with 2012.

The cumulative installed grid-connected PV capacity increased to 12.1 GW_{DC}, 82 percent of which was installed in just the last three years. In 2013, 0.9 GW_{DC} were installed on residential buildings, 1.0 GW_{DC} at non-residential sites, and 2.7 GW_{DC} in the utility sector.

Some PV installations are off-grid, and are power facilities that are too expensive to connect to the grid, such as cabins, telecommunications facilities and road signs. Based on anecdotal information, the size of this market is very small compared with grid-connected installations. IREC has not collected data for off-grid installations, and they are not included in this report's charts.

Almost 155,000 grid-connected PV installations were completed in 2013, a 64 percent increase over the number of installations in 2012. Residential systems accounted for 94 percent of these individual installations. By contrast, residential systems accounted for only 19 percent of the PV capacity installed in 2013. At the end of 2013, 471,000 PV installations were connected to the US grid, including 420,000 residential installations.

Important Factors Driving 2013 Installation Growth Vary by Sector and State

- Federal ITC. The federal ITC remained stable at 30 percent, which means the owner can claim a tax credit of 30 percent of the project cost. Additionally, the accelerated depreciation schedule for commercial installations was unchanged. Tax credits for both residential and commercial installations are set to continue at current levels through the end of 2016, when the residential ITC will expire and the commercial ITC will revert from 30 percent to 10 percent. With this stable incentive, developers and installers can plan and market their products, and consumers can make rational decisions without arbitrary incentive deadlines.

- Lower Installed Costs. The total installed cost for distributed PV installations fell 11 percent in 2013 and has fallen 44 percent over the past four years. The cost decline is even greater for utility installations. Falling module costs is the primary reason for cost declines over the long-term, but all cost components have fallen, including inverter costs and soft costs such as permitting.

- Federal Cash Grants. In February 2009, as part of the American Recovery and Reinvestment Act (ARRA), Congress enacted the US Treasury Grant in Lieu of Tax Credits Program. This program, commonly known as the 1603 Treasury Grant Program, provided commercial installations with the alternative of a cash grant instead of the tax credit. The program was originally scheduled to expire at the end of 2010, but was extended through the end of 2012. The expiration of this program inspired many project developers to begin construction late in 2012 in order to qualify, with project completion scheduled in 2013 through 2016. In 2013, 981 completed solar electric projects were awarded $1.8 billion in cash grants (Treasury 2014). These totals reflect 70 percent fewer projects and 16 percent fewer grant dollars than the 2012 totals. Solar projects received 41 percent of 1603 Treasury Grant funding in 2013, compared with only 17 percent in 2011.

- State RPS Requirements. States encourage investments in utility-scale solar plants with Renewable Portfolio Standard (RPS) policies. An RPS generally requires utilities to generate or procure a certain percentage of electricity from renewable energy. Some states have a "solar carve-out" that also requires a certain percentage of the renewable generation come from solar energy. The terms of each state's RPS are different, but this policy is generally most important for utility-sector installations. In some states, RPS guidelines have led to solar renewable energy credit (SREC) markets, which in turn have resulted in increased demand for and installation of distributed solar. SREC markets are most developed in the Mid-Atlantic states and in Massachusetts. Of the 11 states and territories with more than 10 MW of utility sector installations in 2013, nine have an RPS, usually with a solar carve-out.

- Federal Loan Guarantees. As part of ARRA, the US Department of Energy was authorized to offer loan guarantees for renewable energy and other energy projects. The program expired in September 2011, but projects that received loan guarantees by that date are still being completed. In 2013, all three CSP installations and three of the four largest PV installations received $7.2 billion in loan guarantees from this program for at least a portion of the project's capital cost.
- Third-Party Ownership. The dominant ownership model for utility and non-residential distributed installations has long been third-party ownership. In recent years, this ownership model has expanded to the residential sector, and is now the dominant ownership model in all sectors. This structure may take the form of a lease or a power purchase agreement (PPA). In each case, a third party owns the system, and the system user makes regular payments to the owner. For distributed systems, the system is located at the consumer's facility or home, and the consumer uses the electricity generated on-site. Under third-party ownership, the consumer avoids paying the large up-front capital cost of a PV system.
- Net Metering. Net metering is a simple option for consumers to offset their monthly electricity bills by producing their own energy. It allows customers to send excess energy from an on-site renewable energy system back to the grid, and receive a 1:1 kilowatt-hour credit for that energy. In 2013, 95 percent of distributed installed capacity was net-metered.
- State and Utility Rebates. State and utility financial incentives have historically been one of the most important factors driving PV growth, especially for residential and commercial distributed installations. However, the importance of rebates

is declining. The impact of these rebates varies greatly from state to state. As the cost of PV installations has decreased, rebate levels have dropped and some states have eliminated rebate programs altogether. The largest rebate program in the country, the California Solar Initiative (CSI), methodically reduced rebates for years. Although rebates for this program ended in 2013, PV markets continue to grow in California.

[…]

Information on Top State Markets

PV market activity often has more to do with state policies and incentives than with the amount of available sunlight or solar resource. Most of the top states for grid-connected PV have favorable solar policies. Electricity prices are also a factor; many installations are in states with higher than average prices. As solar prices fall, electricity prices and rate policies become an increasingly important factor in state markets. This section describes the market conditions in the states with the largest number of installations.

California is the most important market for solar in the United States. In 2013, 57 percent of PV capacity, and 67 percent of CSP capacity installed were in California. All market sectors are strong in California.

California has an RPS requirement of 20 percent by 2013, and 33 percent by 2020. This policy includes all renewable technologies, and it inspired many PV installations in 2013. This requirement led to 1.9 GW_{DC}[1] of utility sector PV solar installations in California in 2013. In addition, a 145 MW_{DC} utility PV installation in Arizona supplies electricity for California, and two CSP plants totaling 516 MW_{AC} also supply electricity. A full 76 percent of all utility sector capacity installed in 2013 was either in California or supplies electricity for the California market.

California is also a leader in distributed installations. In 2007, California launched the $3 billion *Go Solar California* campaign.

The largest part of this campaign is the California Solar Initiative (CSI), overseen by the California Public Utilities Commission (CPUC). The CSI awards rebates and performance-based incentives to customers serviced by the state's three investor-owned electric utilities: PG&E, SCE and SDG&E. With $158 million in CSI incentives, more than 375 MW_{DC} of distributed PV were installed in 2013 through this program. Program incentives are based on actual system performance of larger systems and expected system performance of smaller systems. The program stopped accepting new applications in 2013, but systems with reservations may still be installed in the future. Incentive levels were reduced over the duration of the program in 10 "steps," based on the aggregate capacity of PV installed. The average incentive paid per watt in 2013 was 81 percent lower than the average incentive paid in 2007, the first year of the program. The CSI was prudently designed as a long-term program, so the industry in California could rely on long-term policy stability. Because the incentives stepped down over time, the transition to an incentive-free market has been smooth. Even though the CSI incentives are coming to a close, PV installations continue to increase. California's steep, tiered electric rate schedule and large peak period time-of-use rates, combined with net metering, provide enough of an incentive for consumers to continue to install PV systems.

In addition, the California Energy Commission (CEC) administers the New Solar Home Partnership Program for PV installations on new homes, and the CPUC manages the Multi-Family Affordable Solar Housing and the Single-Family Affordable Solar Housing Programs. California's municipal utilities have also installed and incentivized the installation of many systems. The capacity of distributed installations by California public utilities increased by 48 percent to 125 MW_{DC} in 2013.

The result of these programs is that 35 percent of all 2013 distributed PV capacity installed in the US was in California.

California has long had strong incentives and a solid net metering policy. Now, as incentives are dwindling, dropping PV prices and high electricity rates are propelling continued sustained growth in distributed installations.

Arizona ranks second for PV capacity installed in 2013, though the capacity installed was 42 percent less than what was installed in 2012. The 250 MW$_{AC}$ Solana Generating Station, a CSP plant, was completed in 2013. However, the numbers are skewed because some of the utility PV capacity installed in Arizona supplied electricity to California utilities. If only installations in Arizona that supply electricity for Arizona are considered, the state would still rank number two, and the decline in PV capacity installed would be a much more modest five percent. Installation of distributed PV increased by 31 percent in 2013. Including the CSP plant means that Arizona shows significant solar growth in 2013.

Arizona's current RPS requires that 15 percent of electricity must be generated from renewable sources by 2025. Distributed generation must provide 30 percent of that energy, divided equally among residential and non-utility, non-residential installations. Solar water heaters may also provide RECs for RPS compliance in Arizona. Starting in 2014, new residential PV customers of Arizona Public Service will pay a fee of $.70 per kilowatt to participate in net metering.

In New Jersey, an RPS with a solar carve-out has built a strong PV market. The solar requirement was 306 GWh in 2011, increasing to 5,316 GWh in 2026. In the early years of New Jersey's PV growth, rebates were the most important driver, peaking in 2006 at $78 million in expenditures. In 2013, only two residual rebates were granted. New Jersey's capacity-based rebate program has been converted into a performance-based incentive that involves payments based on the actual energy production of a PV system. This performance-based program created a market for SRECs, which New Jersey utilities use to comply with the RPS. However, New Jersey SREC prices crashed in 2012, falling to less than half the price that had been seen in previous years. The state made policy changes to stabilize its long-term SREC market. Even so, the new PV capacity installed in 2013 fell by over 50 percent compared with 2012. New Jersey was the number two state market for many years, but it fell to number three in 2012 and to number five in 2013.

North Carolina has an RPS with a 0.2 percent solar carve-out by 2018. North Carolina also has a 35 percent state tax credit, one of the highest tax credits in the country. Most North Carolina PV system owners sell the electricity generated to utility companies or, until recently, to NC GreenPower. North Carolina has established a system to track RECs and record compliance with the state's RPS and solar carve-out.

Massachusetts has a long history of providing rebates for PV installations. In 2010, Massachusetts awarded $37 million in rebates for 14 MW_{DC} of PV installations. These installations represented 63 percent of the PV capacity installed in Massachusetts that year. In 2013, the state awarded $5.5 million in rebates for 15 MW_{DC} of PV installations. Thus, 87 percent fewer rebate dollars funded seven percent more installed PV capacity. During the same period, the amount of installed capacity *not* supported by rebates increased from 9 MW_{DC} to 208 MW_{DC}. This can be attributed to the Massachusetts RPS, which has a solar carve-out of 0.163 percent in 2012 and 0.2744 percent in 2013. Massachusetts uses an SREC market for compliance with the RPS requirements.

Hawaii has the highest electricity rates in the country. The 2013 average price of nearly $0.33/kWh is more than twice the rate in any other state, and almost three-and-a-half times the national average electricity price. Hawaii also has a personal state solar income tax credit. Some 92 percent of Hawaii installations were distributed in 2013. The financial benefits of PV are more favorable in Hawaii than in any other state. On a per capita basis, Hawaii had, by far, the most installed capacity of distributed PV.

Georgia had the highest growth in PV capacity installed of any top state, with 10 times the capacity installed in 2013 compared with 2012. In 2012, the Georgia Public Service Commission approved the Georgia Power Advanced Solar Initiative. This authorizes Georgia Power to purchase up to 90 MW of distributed installations from small and medium size projects and 120 MW from utility scale projects. In 2013, 22 MW_{DC} of distributed installations and 58 MW_{DC} of utility installations were installed through this program.

In New York, the New York State Energy Research and Development Authority and the Long Island Power Authority have operated long-term significant rebate programs. New York also has a customer-sited carve-out under its RPS Program that funds many of the current NY policy initiatives. Because of these programs, installations have increased steadily over the years.

[…]

Prospects for the Future

What can we expect for the future of US solar markets? The short-term prospects for continued strong growth are good. As the federal ITC expires for residential installations and declines for commercial installations at the end of 2016, we can expect that implicit deadline to have both positive and negative impacts on the market.

Growth continues in the residential sector. Although the market is concentrated in several states, many states have growing numbers of homeowners installing solar. The future of net metering will be studied in many states, and the outcomes of numerous cost/benefit studies and policy debates will affect residential markets.

The non-residential distributed PV sector was the weakest sector in 2013, and that trend will likely continue. Changes to the New Jersey program made in 2012 will help stabilize the market in that important state and may help fuel modest growth in 2014.

Numerous utility PV projects under construction or approved mean that this sector will continue to grow in 2014. However, the growth in this sector is extremely concentrated in a few states. As those states meet their RPS requirements, future installations will need to be justified on economics. The slow growth of US electricity consumption means that most utilities will not be aggressively pursuing new power options.

Concentrating solar power projects face a similar market dynamic. A number of plants are under construction and will be completed over the next few years. New orders will require a different market model than installations in the pipeline now.

[…]

Clean Energy Soared in the US in 2017

Erica Gies

An independent reporter who covers science and the environment, Erica Gies writes for Inside Climate News, *a Pulitzer Prize-winning nonpartisan news organization that is dedicated to covering climate change, energy, and the environment.*

As President Donald Trump moved to roll back environmental protections and foster a boom in fossil fuel energy production, his administration effectively abandoned the race for global leadership in slowing global warming.

But in many ways, the transformation of the energy economy in a new, green direction continued apace in the United States, just as abroad.

Some pre-Trump policies, like US tax breaks for renewables, survived. The social and market forces that have been shouldering coal aside persisted. And the mantle of leadership passed not only to Europe, China and developing nations, but to American cities and states.

The cost of renewable energy keeps going down, comparing favorably with coal. Battery technology also continues to improve and get cheaper. And digital technology is making electric markets cleaner and more efficient, as well.

Here are how these trends are emerging, both in the United States and abroad.

Coal: It's Closing Time

Trump famously promised to bring back coal, and he's been trying. At the U.N. climate conference in Bonn in November, the only official US event promoted "clean" fossil fuels as a solution to climate change. Trump's proposed rollback of the Clean Power

"Clean Energy Soared in the US in 2017 Due to Economics, Policy and Technology," by Erica Gies, Inside Climate News, January 3, 2018. Reprinted by permission.

Plan would retract stringent limits on emissions from coal plants. Energy secretary Rick Perry told the Federal Energy Regulatory Commission to "fix" grid resiliency by requiring some power plants to maintain larger on-site reserves of coal and nuclear fuel—a strategy widely derided.

Signs of coal's demise are everywhere. More than half of the coal plants in the United States have closed since 2010, and coal's market share continues to decline rapidly, according to a new report from UK-based Carbon Tracker, an independent financial think tank. It concludes that "new coal capacity is not remotely competitive" and, in the next few years, building new power plants that use natural gas and renewables will often be cheaper than continuing to operate existing coal plants.

The economics are just as unfavorable for coal in Europe. Another recent report from Carbon Tracker found more than half of coal plants there are losing money. By 2030, almost all will be, thanks to tougher air pollution protections and higher carbon prices. Soon it will be cheaper to build new solar and wind generation than to continue running existing coal plants, the report found. The United Kingdom has slashed its coal usage from 40 percent of the nation's electricity to 2 percent in the last five years. Australia and China are also among the countries that shut down coal plants or canceled plans for new ones.

More and more places around the world, including China and India, are deciding that air pollution impacts on human health must be controlled, requiring costly scrubbers and filters that increase the cost of coal generation. At the same time, prices for other energy sources have stayed low—including natural gas due to copious fracking in the United States, and wind and solar, which are continuing their steep decline due to economies of scale and technological improvements.

Even the International Energy Agency (IEA), known for its myopic view of fossil fuels and routine underestimates of renewable energy growth, discerns this trend. Renewable energy's "explosive growth in the power sector marks the end of the boom years for coal," says its latest World Energy Outlook, predicting that renewables will capture two-thirds of global investment and generate 40 percent of total power in 2040 "as they become, for many countries, the least-cost source of new generation."

Renewables Are Competing on Price

In fact, renewables are already the cheaper option in many places. The IEA's 2017 Energy Outlook notes that, since 2010, costs of new solar PV have come down by 70 percent and wind by 25 percent. And China's energy agency announced last January that it intends to spend at least $360 billion on renewable energy by 2020. It's that kind of investment that is helping to bring prices down worldwide.

Just 18 months ago, Zambia made headlines when a World Bank-led solar power auction saw a winning bid of 6.02 cents per kilowatt-hour. In October this year, Saudi Arabia saw a solar price of 1.79 cents per kilowatt-hour, and in November, Mexico saw 1.77 cents per kilowatt-hour for wind. Even in surprising corners such as Alberta, home to Canada's oil sands and coal mines, the province's first wind auction saw a winning price of 3.7 cents per kilowatt hour, half the cost of new natural gas generation there.

These prices are turning heads. In 2016, renewable energy accounted for almost two-thirds of new power capacity globally, and this was another record year. The IEA expects that domination to continue, at least through 2022. That's true in the United States as well. Renewables have been the majority of added capacity since 2014, despite this year's solar dramas such as lobbying for tariffs on cheaper Chinese panels and industry shakeups.

US wind and solar also emerged only lightly scratched by the Republican tax cut, after tax credits were in the crosshairs. Republicans buckled under pressure from red states like Texas, where a new wind facility that opened in December pushed the state's wind capacity past coal.

Aside from what happens at the federal level, states continued with their strong commitments. For example, California's Public Utilities Commission reported that it is well ahead of its target to get 33 percent of its power from renewables by 2020 and appears on track to meet the 2030 target of 50 percent by 2020. Gov. Jerry Brown, seizing on that momentum, is now advocating that the state hit 100 percent by 2040.

Batteries: Cheaper and Better

Renewables' strong growth demands more energy storage to avoid dumping wind and solar power that can't be used immediately, and regulators are increasingly aware of storage's value in supporting the modern grid. It helps that adding storage is now more feasible because battery prices have come down by 40 percent since 2010, according to the IEA's 2017 Energy Outlook. Water storage via pumped hydro and regulated dam use are also supporting wind and solar, along with "virtual storage" such as demand response.

Lithium-ion batteries used for grid storage, vehicles and home storage have been getting incrementally better and cheaper, both from economies of scale and technological advances. Meanwhile, innovation continues in other battery technologies. The progress led to a flurry of new electric vehicles and manufacturer and country commitments to phasing out internal combustion engines. Even trucking is beginning to go electric.

A report from Bloomberg New Energy Finance predicted in November that the energy storage market will double six times between 2016 and 2030. This boom will mirror solar's rise from 2000 to 2015, the report said, in which the share of solar as a percentage of energy generation doubled seven times. In the US, states are following California's lead, which first set a storage target in 2013. Now 21 states have storage targets or are planning projects.

Lithium-ion batteries are even beginning to compete on price with natural gas peaker plants, the older, dirtier power plants that currently supply electricity when demand spikes. This month the California Public Utilities Commission is set to vote on a plan to replace three natural gas-fired power plants with energy storage. Experts say this could be the beginning of the end for peaker plants.

Digitalization of Electricity

As solar, wind, storage, and other new energy resources such as electric vehicles and smart appliances come onto the grid, supply is more variable and transactions—moving and paying for energy—are going in both directions. These changes make grid management and the delivery of reliable electricity challenging.

Increasingly, grid managers are using vast reams of data; powerful analytics, including machine learning; and widespread connectivity, including machine-to-machine communication to make energy systems more flexible, efficient, and reliable, a trend the IEA covered in a special report on digitalization and energy.

These systems can optimize myriad variables in real time. For example, they can store solar power generated in the afternoon for later use when people get home from work, or they can send wind power from the desert to the city, or they can shave tiny amounts of electricity delivery from multiple customers via their smart appliances, aggregating enough to not turn on a peaker plant. The IEA report found that, by 2040, demand response could provide 185 gigawatts of system flexibility, roughly equivalent to the supply capacity of Australia and Italy combined, saving $270 billion in new electricity infrastructure.

Electric vehicles' batteries can be used as storage for the grid, and energy digitalization can shift cars' charging to times when electricity demand is low and supply is high. Doing so could save $100 billion to $280 billion in avoided investment in new electricity infrastructure between 2016 and 2040, according to the IEA report. Improving analytics and AI can also create more accurate forecasts for wind and solar, allow grid managers to better capture that energy and reduce fossil fuel use.

This is the future of energy, and it's coming much faster than conventional wisdom predicted. Deals between data and artificial intelligence startups and energy companies increased 10-fold in 2017, according to accountancy firm BDO. Altogether, these policies, technologies, and markets are overcoming hurdles to new types of greener energy—solar, wind, storage, efficiency— decreasing greenhouse gas emissions from electricity.

It may prove impossible for those who favor fossil fuels to turn back the gears of progress.

CHAPTER 2

| Is Clean Energy Affordable?

Green and Low-Cost Energy from Inexhaustible Sources

RESET

RESET is an organization dedicated to digital and social innovations for sustainable development, with a focus on implementing smart solutions to create positive social change.

Energy resources exist in different forms—some exist as stocks and are exhaustible, others exist as flows and are inexhaustible. The effects of climate change, and the impact that greenhouse gas emissions have on the atmosphere, are ushering in a reassessment of where our energy supply comes from and, more importantly, how sustainable it is.

The first form mentioned above is fossil fuels such as petroleum and carbon energy, the second form relates to resources based on constantly replenishing flows of energy such as solar, wind, hydro and geothermal as well as quantities grown by nature in the form of biomass. All of the latter forms are (mostly) green, clean and renewable and therefore could provide an answer to the shortage in commodities and increasing energy demands. Rising consumption of fossil fuels is still set to drive up greenhouse gas emissions and global temperatures, resulting in potentially catastrophic and irreversible climate change. Alternative energy sources can help to reduce emissions of CO_2.

The possibilities to use renewable energy are still developing: energy resources evolve dynamically as a function of human engineering ingenuity. There is still a lot to do with regards to installing and developing alternative energy production—energy demand is increasing worldwide, day by day with ongoing population growth and industrialisation.

"Renewable Energy—Environmentally Friendly and Low Cost Energy from Inexhaustible Sources," Reset, September 2015. Reprinted by permission.

Why Renewables?

Our reliance upon fossil fuels such as coal and oil is negatively affecting the planet. Burning these fossil fuels increases the amount of carbon dioxide (CO_2) that is released into the atmosphere, leading to a heightened greenhouse effect and warming of the earth. With governments trying to reduce CO_2 emissions, renewable sources of energy (such as those derived from wind, the sun and waves) are presenting themselves as a viable, eco-friendly options to meet the world's energy needs.

US-based organisation the Union of Concerned Scientists did a numbers crunch that shows how much CO_2 is emitted when using conventional forms of power as well as renewable sources.

"Compared with natural gas, which emits between 0.6 and 2 pounds of carbon dioxide equivalent per kilowatt-hour (CO_2E/kWh), and coal, which emits between 1.4 and 3.6 pounds of CO_2E/kWh, wind emits only 0.02 to 0.04 pounds of CO_2E/kWh, solar 0.07 to 0.2, geothermal 0.1 to 0.2, and hydroelectric between 0.1 and 0.5. Renewable electricity generation from biomass can have a wide range of global warming emissions depending on the resource and how it is harvested. Sustainably sourced biomass has a low emissions footprint, while unsustainable sources of biomass can generate significant global warming emissions."

In addition, renewable sources of energy release little or no particles that cause air pollution or negatively impact human health; wind and solar power consume virtually no water (geothermal and biomass require water for plant cooling), meaning the strain on local water supply can be significantly reduced; and sources of renewable energy are, generally speaking, vast and inexhaustible. By contrast, a 2011 study conducted by Harvard Medical Centre concluded that coal costs the US public up to 500 billion USD per year, with many of these costs relating to public health and waste management.

Types of Renewable Energy

Below is a brief outline of the various forms of renewable energy.

Solar

In basic terms, solar power is created by converting sunlight into electricity. The most commonways this occurs is via the installation and use of photovoltaic panels in areas that catch a lot of rays or via concentrated solar power systems.

One of the biggest benefits of solar energy is the inexhaustive, ready availability of the source—the amount of sunlight the earth receives per year makes the sun the most abundant source of energy worldwide, trumping coal and other fossil fuels.

Wind

Wind power has been around in one form or another for centuries— think conventional sail boats and agricultural windmills that pump water. These days, the power of the wind is being harnessed to generate electricity, using massive, tri-bladed, horizontal-axis turbines that stand on towers as tall as a 20 storey building.

The turbines—usually clustered together in so-called wind farms—are planted in areas with high winds and must face into the wind. These modern-day windmills convert kinetic energy into electricity: wind moves the turbine, which triggers and turns a shaft that's connected to a generator that produces electricity.

Wind power is the fastest growing source of electricity in the world.

Hydroelectric Power

Hydroelectric power (sometimes known as hydro power) leverages the power of moving water, regardless of if the water is falling downwards, like a waterfall, or flowing like a stream. To make use of this power, large turbines are fitted with electrical generators. Water passing through the turbines causes them to spin, which sets of the generators that then convert the kinetic energy into electricity. The power of moving water (and therefore the amount of electricity derived from it) is influenced by both the volume and the height difference between the source and the water's outflow and "energy is derived to make power by the force of water moving from a higher elevation to a lower elevation through a large tube otherwise known...as a penstock." (Source: Electricity Forum)

Norway has made great strides in adopting hydro power, with approximately 99 percent of the country's energy needs met via this type of electricity. Hydro power does have some drawbacks namely, the building of dams to accommodate turbines can have a negative impact on local flora and fauna.

Ocean/Tidal Energy

Another form of energy that humans have been making use of for a long time is ocean energy or tidal energy. Regardless, tidal energy represents a relatively small section of the current renewable energy market.

There are three different ways to harness tidal energy: tidal streams (where turbines are placed in fast-flowing bodies of water), barrages (where turbines are placed in dams. The dam gates are open as the tide rises and close when the dam is full, capturing an excess of water that is then run through the turbines) and tidal lagoons (where turbines are placed in pools of sea water hemmed in by natural or man-made barriers).

One of the big benefits of tidal energy is that, unlike other sources, tidal currents are reliably predictable. Depending on the type of generator being used, building and installing the necessary infrastructure can be expensive (barrages), can negatively impact the surrounding environment (tidal streams) or might not produce so much energy (tidal lagoons).

Geothermal Energy

According to the Union of Concerned Scientists, "Below Earth's crust, there is a layer of hot and molten rock, called magma. Heat is continually produced in this layer, mostly from the decay of naturally radioactive materials such as uranium and potassium.

The amount of heat within 10,000 meters (about 33,000 feet) of Earth's surface contains 50,000 times more energy than all the oil and natural gas resources in the world....as of 2013 more than 11,700 megawatts (MW) of large, utility-scale geothermal capacity was in operation globally, with another 11,700 MW in planned capacity additions on the way. These geothermal facilities produced approximately 68 billion kilowatt-hours of electricity, enough to meet the annual needs of more than 6 million typical US households. Geothermal plants account for more than 25 percent of the electricity produced in both Iceland and El Salvador."

Biomass

Derived from organic materials (such as plant and animal materials), biomass releases energy (as heat) when it is burned. Among the general sources for producing biomass power are: wood and forest residues (like bark and sawdust left over from the paper-making process); non-toxic waste (like biodegradable garbage); some crop residues; and manure. These can be burned in biomass power plants to produce steam which then triggers a turbine that produces electricity.

On the downside, the process of burning biomass does release carbon into the atmosphere, meaning that the emissions resulting from biomass must be weighed against the number of emissions that would result from any of power source biomass was looking to replace.

Renewable Energy Worldwide

Talk about the benefits of renewable energy may be rife however, the actual penetration and usage rates still have room to grow. The US Energy Information Administration puts global consumption of electricity from renewable sources at around 11 percent and total electricity generation from renewables at around 21 percent. The obstacles are manifold: lengthy permission procedures, import tariffs and technical barriers, insecure financing of renewable energy projects and insufficient awareness of the opportunities for renewable energy. Worldwide, renewable energy plays no decisive role although it offers clean alternatives to traditional energy sources as well as decentralised energy supply solutions to developing countries.

However, things are beginning to shift. After several years of being pegged as "too expensive," the modern renewable energy industry is now being viewed as a cost-effective, more sustainable competitor to conventional forms of fuel and power generation. Data released by the International Renewable Energy Agency (IRENA) in early 2015 show that most forms of renewable energy have now achieved price parity with coal and some are even cheaper. "Any remaining perceptions that renewable power generation technologies are expensive or uncompetitive are at best outdated, and at worst a dangerous fallacy," stated Adnan Z. Amin, the director-general of IRENA.

"Renewable energy projects across the globe are now matching or outperforming fossil fuels, particularly when accounting for externalities like local pollution, environmental damage and ill health."

The world's largest investor in renewable energy is China. As the world's biggest importer of oil, largest consumer of energy and home to some of the worst air pollution, China is uniquely placed to drive adoption rates of renewable energy. According to Clean Technica, "By 2014, China had created generating capacity from water, wind and solar sources of 378 GW—as compared with 172 GW for the US, 84 GW for Germany, and 71 GW for India."

The European Union has set itself a mandate to fulfill 20 percent of its energy needs with renewable energy by 2020. Some countries within the EU have more tailored, loftier goals in mind such as Denmark, which aims to derive 70 percent of its electricity from renewable sources by 2020 and 100 percent by 2050.

A recent report from the US Energy Information Administration predicted that renewable sources of energy, including solar and wind, could be the fastest-growing sources of power until at least 2040. Since 2004, investment into the renewable sector has grown more than five times while the uptake and installation of photovoltaic systems continues to grow year after year.

The largest solar farm in Africa, the Jasper PV Project located in South Africa, was completed in October 2014, with the capacity to to deliver 180,000 megawatt-hours of electricity every year to over 80,000 homes. In mid-2015, the Africa Progress Panel launched a report that set out a plan to make electricity accessible to every single person on the African continent by 2030. The report, titled "Power, People, Planet, Africa," called for this to be done with renewable electricity, effectively asking leaders of African nations to leapfrog using fossil fuels. The Africa Progress Panel aims to provide low-cost solar panels that would make energy accessible to the 621 million people lacking access to electricity today. The estimated amount of money needed is 55 billion USD. According to the Panel, half this amount could be generated from within the African continent by increasing sub-Saharan Africa's tax-to GDP ratio by one percent of GDP. Another 20 billion would come from a new "connectivity fund" of which half would come from Africa itself and another half from bilateral aid.

Connecting everyone in Africa to electricity and simultaneously making that electricity renewable is, however, easier said than done. According to a publication by the International Renewable Energy Agency (IRENA), it is currently more difficult to obtain financing for renewable energy power plants than for fossil fuel plants.

Everything Has Two Sides

Renewable energy sources can be useful and cause damage at the same time. One must always look at the whole picture. The use of alternative energy resources has to be evaluated by its eco-balance.

For example, heavy metals are used for the production of solar power cells which remain in the factory, though the finished solar module isn't toxic at all. In response to this, scientists are researching and developing more sustainable methods of making solar cells, such as recyclable cells made out of trees.

Windparks are not without their controversies due to the irritation they can cause to birds and bats. Offshore windparks could be a problem for migratory birds.

Diverse hydroelectric power plants can also cause changes in existing ecosystems. Burning biomass can produce nitrogen monoxide, sulfur dioxide and respirable dust.

Using geothermal energy fluids drawn from the deep earth carry a toxic and explosive mixture of gases, notably carbon dioxide, hydrogen sulfide, methane and ammonia. Plant construction can adversely affect land stability.

The Future

Rising energy prices, increased import dependence and rising greenhouse-gas emissions are environmentally, economically and socially unsustainable. Achieving a more secure, low-carbon energy system calls for radical action by governments at national and local levels, and through participation in coordinated international mechanisms. Greater reliance on renewable energy sources offers enormous economic, social, and environmental benefits. As seen in many countries, developing and implementing alternative energy resources can provide a lot of jobs.

With centralised power, be it through coal, hydro or nuclear power, electrifying cities is the priority and rural villages, often at the tail end of the power grid, are literally left in the dark. Locally installed power plants for wind power, solar energy or biomass are decentralised sources of energy and thereby empower people at a grassroots level. It creates independence of power companies and low-cost options to bring energy to rural areas.

A first step at international level is the funding of the International Energy Agency IEA. 136 countries are part of it. IEA assumes that renewable energy could cover more than one fourth of the world's primary energy demand by 2030.

Debunking the Myth That Coal Is Cheap

Gary Cohen

Gary Cohen was the policy director and chief administrator of the National Toxics Campaign and chief administrator of the National Toxics Campaign Fund. He also wrote and researched for the organization, which was dedicated to helping local communities seek environmental justice.

In May, Republican US Sen. Shelley Moore Capito of West Virginia introduced legislation to roll back President Obama's Clean Power Plan. Proposed by the Environmental Protection Agency in 2014, the plan would require states to reduce air pollution and carbon dioxide emissions and would likely speed the retirement of older, inefficient coal-fired power plants.

Capito, Senate Majority Leader Mitch McConnell of Kentucky and other lawmakers from coal country view the Clean Power Plan as an existential threat to their states' economies. They contend that phasing out coal would remove a cheap source of energy, leading to higher costs for utility ratepayers.

Here's the problem with that argument: Coal is only cheap if you choose to ignore its staggering costs to human health and the environment.

Just last month, a report from the International Monetary Fund (hardly a radical outfit) found that the environmental, health and other costs of burning fossil fuels reach $5.3 trillion a year—$10 million every minute. Coal—the dirtiest fuel in terms of air pollution and climate-warming carbon emissions—accounts for just over half that total. By shouldering these costs, we are, in effect, granting a massive public subsidy to coal and other fossil-fuel companies.

Health costs from air pollution account for nearly half of that $5.3 trillion subsidy. Those costs include the burden of care for

From "The Myth That Coal is Cheap" by Gary Cohen. Reproduced by permission of Island Press, Washington, DC. August 23, 2016.

cancer and respiratory and heart disease as well as lost wages due to disability and death. Those costs are paid by each and every one of us, in days of missed work and nights spent in the emergency room, in higher tax rates and in soaring insurance premiums. Some pay the ultimate price: A recent study by researchers at the Massachusetts Institute of Technology found that air pollution from US coal-power plants causes more than 50,000 premature deaths each year. Most of those deaths are in the east-central US and in the Midwest, where power plants burn high-sulfur coal.

Worse, the health costs of coal fall most heavily on those who can least afford them. The dirtiest coal plants are disproportionately located in low-income communities of color, which is one reason that African Americans' rates of asthma are 35 percent higher than among Caucasians.

And then there are the steep and growing costs of adapting to a changing climate. The societal costs of climate change—droughts, flooding, wildfires and superstorms—have reached $1.27 trillion a year, according to the International Monetary Fund report. Coal produces more than its share of climate-changing carbon emissions: While coal-fired plants supply just 40 percent of the nation's electricity, they account for more than three quarters of carbon-dioxide emissions from power generation. Again, when you consider the mounting costs of climate change, the greatest burden is borne by the most vulnerable people.

Coal, then, is anything but cheap, despite what you might hear from industry executives and their friends in Congress.

Of course, we expect industries to defend their interests. A generation ago, the tobacco industry and congressional delegations from tobacco-growing states denied the health impacts of smoking and fought to protect public farm subsidies for tobacco growers. But eventually the societal cost of smoking became too great to bear and the subsidies were revoked.

It's time to do the same for coal. Just as we refused to subsidize tobacco, we can stop propping up the coal industry. The Clean

Power Plan is a good start; a carbon tax that captured the full health and environmental costs of fossil fuels would be even better.

Market forces have sealed coal's fate in the long term. Coal-fired power plants are already being made obsolete by renewables such as wind and solar. In 2014, there were more jobs created in the renewable sector than in fossil fuels. By removing public subsidies for coal, we can speed the transition to a clean-energy future rather than doubling down on the dirty and costly fuel of the past.

The Advantages of Wind Energy

US Department of Energy

The US Department of Energy and the Office of Energy Efficiency &
Renewable Energy are dedicated to using their investments to make
clean energy technologies and services more available and reliable
while also lowering costs for both energy users and society as a whole.

Wind energy offers many advantages, which explains why it's one of the fastest-growing energy sources in the world. Research efforts are aimed at addressing the challenges to greater use of wind energy. Read on to learn more about the benefits of wind power and some of the challenges it is working to overcome.

Advantages of Wind Power

- Wind power is cost-effective. Land-based utility-scale wind is one of the lowest-priced energy sources available today, costing between two and six cents per kilowatt-hour, depending on the wind resource and the particular project's financing. Because the electricity from wind farms is sold at a fixed price over a long period of time (e.g. 20+ years) and its fuel is free, wind energy mitigates the price uncertainty that fuel costs add to traditional sources of energy.
- Wind creates jobs. The US wind sector employed more than 100,000 workers in 2016, and wind turbine technician is one of the fastest-growing American jobs of the decade. According to the *Wind Vision Report*, wind has the potential to support more than 600,000 jobs in manufacturing, installation, maintenance, and supporting services by 2050.
- Wind enables US industry growth and US competitiveness. Wind has an annual economic impact of about $20 billion on the US economy, The United States has a vast domestic

"Advantages and Challenges of Wind Energy," US Department of Energy.

resources and a highly-skilled workforce, and can compete globally in the clean energy economy.

- It's a clean fuel source. Wind energy doesn't pollute the air like power plants that rely on combustion of fossil fuels, such as coal or natural gas, which emit particulate matter, nitrogen oxides, and sulfur dioxide—causing human health problems and economic damages. Wind turbines don't produce atmospheric emissions that cause acid rain, smog, or greenhouse gases.

- Wind is a domestic source of energy. The nation's wind supply is abundant and inexhaustible. Over the past 10 years, cumulative wind power capacity in the United States increased an average of 30% per year, and wind now has the largest renewable generation capacity of all renewables in the United States.

- It's sustainable. Wind is actually a form of solar energy. Winds are caused by the heating of the atmosphere by the sun, the rotation of the Earth, and the Earth's surface irregularities. For as long as the sun shines and the wind blows, the energy produced can be harnessed to send power across the grid.

- Wind turbines can be built on existing farms or ranches. This greatly benefits the economy in rural areas, where most of the best wind sites are found. Farmers and ranchers can continue to work the land because the wind turbines use only a fraction of the land. Wind power plant owners make rent payments to the farmer or rancher for the use of the land, providing landowners with additional income.

Challenges of Wind Power

- Wind power must still compete with conventional generation sources on a cost basis. Depending on how energetic a wind site is, the wind farm might not be cost competitive. Even though the cost of wind power has decreased dramatically in the past 10 years, the technology requires a higher initial investment than fossil-fueled generators.

- Good wind sites are often located in remote locations, far from cities where the electricity is needed. Transmission lines must be built to bring the electricity from the wind farm to the city. However, building just a few already-proposed transmission lines could significantly reduce the costs of expanding wind energy.

- Wind resource development might not be the most profitable use of the land. Land suitable for wind-turbine installation must compete with alternative uses for the land, which might be more highly valued than electricity generation.

- Turbines might cause noise and aesthetic pollution. Although wind power plants have relatively little impact on the environment compared to conventional power plants, concern exists over the noise produced by the turbine blades and visual impacts to the landscape.

- Turbine blades could damage local wildlife. Birds have been killed by flying into spinning turbine blades. Most of these problems have been resolved or greatly reduced through technological development or by properly siting wind plants.

Barriers to Renewable Energy

Union of Concerned Scientists

The Union of Concerned Scientists develops and implements innovative and practical solutions to the planet's most pressing problems, including global warming, finding sustainable methods of food development and transport, and reducing the threat of nuclear war.

I n March 2017, wind and solar accounted for 10 percent of all US electricity generation for the first time *ever*. Although 10 percent may not sound high, it reflected a major achievement for both technologies, which have overcome numerous barriers to become competitive with coal, natural gas, and nuclear power.

But renewables still face major obstacles. Some are inherent with all new technologies; others are the result of a skewed regulatory framework and marketplace. This page explores the barriers to renewable energy in detail, with a focus on wind and solar.

Capital Costs

The most obvious and widely publicized barrier to renewable energy is cost—specifically, capital costs, or the upfront expense of building and installing solar and wind farms. Like most renewables, solar and wind are exceedingly cheap to operate—their "fuel" is free, and maintenance is minimal—so the bulk of the expense comes from building the technology.

The average cost in 2017 to install solar systems ranged from a little over $2,000 per kilowatt (kilowatts are a measure of power capacity) for large-scale systems to almost $3,700 for residential systems. A new natural gas plant might have costs around $1,000/kW. Wind comes in around $1,200 to $1,700/kw.

"Barriers to Renewable Energy Technologies," Union of Concerned Scientists (WWW. UCSUSA.ORG), December 20, 2017. Reprinted by permission.

Higher construction costs might make financial institutions more likely to perceive renewables as risky, lending money at higher rates and making it harder for utilities or developers to justify the investment. For natural gas and other fossil fuel power plants, the cost of fuel may be passed onto the consumer, lowering the risk associated with the initial investment (though increasing the risk of erratic electric bills).

However, if costs over the *lifespan* of energy projects are taken into account, wind and utility-scale solar can be the least expensive energy generating sources, according to asset management company Lazard. As of 2017, the cost (before tax credits that would further drop the costs) of wind power was $30-60 per megawatt-hour (a measure of energy), and large-scale solar cost $43-53/MWh. For comparison: energy from the most efficient type of natural gas plants cost $42-78/MWh; coal power cost at least $60/MWh.

Even more encouragingly, renewable energy capital costs have fallen dramatically since the early 2000s, and will likely continue to do so. For example: between 2006 and 2016, the average value of photovoltaic modules themselves plummeted from $3.50/watt $0.72/watt—an 80 percent decrease in only 10 years.

Siting and Transmission

Nuclear power, coal, and natural gas are all highly *centralized* sources of power, meaning they rely on relatively few high output power plants. Wind and solar, on the other hand, offer a *decentralized* model, in which smaller generating stations, spread across a large area, work together to provide power.

Decentralization offers a few key advantages (including, importantly, grid resilience), but it also presents barriers: siting and transmission.

Siting is the need to locate things like wind turbines and solar farms on pieces of land. Doing so requires negotiations, contracts, permits, and community relations, all of which can increase costs and delay or kill projects.

Transmission refers to the power lines and infrastructure needed to move electricity from where it's generated to where it's consumed. Because wind and solar are relative newcomers, most of what exists today was built to serve large fossil fuel and nuclear power plants.

But wind and solar farms aren't all sited near old nuclear or fossil fuel power plants (in fact, some areas with fewer older power plants, such as the Great Plains and Southwest, offer some of the country's best renewable potential). To adequately take advantage of these resources, new transmission infrastructure is needed—and transmission costs money, and needs to be sited. Both the financing and the siting can be significant barriers for developers and customers, even when they're eager for more renewables—though, again, clean energy momentum is making this calculation easier.

Market Entry

For most of the last century US electricity was dominated by certain major players, including coal, nuclear, and, most recently, natural gas. Utilities across the country have invested heavily in these technologies, which are very mature and well understood, and which hold enormous market power.

This situation—the well-established nature of existing technologies—presents a formidable barrier for renewable energy. Solar, wind, and other renewable resources need to compete with wealthier industries that benefit from existing infrastructure, expertise, and policy. It's a difficult market to enter.

New energy technologies—startups—face even larger barriers. They compete with major market players like coal and gas, *and* with proven, low-cost solar and wind technologies. To prove their worth, they must demonstrate scale: most investors want large quantities of energy, ideally at times when wind and solar aren't available. That's difficult to accomplish, and a major reason why new technologies suffer high rates of failure.

Increased government investment in clean energy—in the form of subsidies, loan assistance, and research and development—would help.

Unequal Playing Field

You don't tend to see multi-billion dollar industries without also seeing outsized political influence—and the fossil fuel industry is no exception.

Oil Change International estimates that the United States spends $37.5 billion on subsidies for fossil fuels *every year*. Through direct subsidies, tax breaks, and other incentives and loopholes, US taxpayers help fund the industry's research and development, mining, drilling, and electricity generation. While subsidies have likely increased domestic production, they've also diverted capital from more productive activities (such as energy efficiency) and constrained the growth of renewable energy (solar and wind enjoy fewer subsidies and, generally, receive much less preferential political treatment).

For decades, the fossil fuel industry has used its influence to spread false or misleading information about climate change—a strong motivation for choosing low-carbon energy sources like wind or solar (in addition to the economic reasons). Industry leaders knew about the risks of global warming as early as the 1970s, but recognized that dealing with global warming meant using fewer fossil fuels. They went on to finance—and continue to fund—climate disinformation campaigns, aimed at sewing doubt about climate change and renewable energy.

Their efforts were successful. Despite widespread scientific consensus, climate action is now a partisan issue in the US Congress, complicating efforts to move from fossil fuels to clean energy.

The disconnect between science and policy means that the price we pay for coal and gas *isn't* representative of the true cost of fossil fuels (ie, it doesn't reflect the enormous costs of global warming and other externalities). This in turn means that renewables aren't entering an equal playing field: they're competing with industries that we subsidize both directly (via government incentives) and indirectly (by not punishing polluters).

Emission fees or caps on total pollution, potentially with tradable emission permits, are examples of ways we could use to help remove this barrier.

Reliability Misconceptions

Renewable energy opponents love to highlight the variability of the sun and wind as a way of bolstering support for coal, gas, and nuclear plants, which can more easily operate on-demand or provide "baseload" (continuous) power. The argument is used to undermine large investments in renewable energy, presenting a rhetorical barrier to higher rates of wind and solar adoption.

But reality is much more favorable for clean energy. Solar and wind are highly predictable, and when spread across a large enough geographic area—and paired with complementary generation sources—become highly reliable. Modern grid technologies like advanced batteries, real-time pricing, and smart appliances can also help solar and wind be essential elements of a well-performing grid.

Tests performed in California, which has some of the highest rates of renewable electricity use in the world, provide real-world validation for the idea that solar and wind can actually *enhance* grid reliability. A 2017 Department of Energy report confirmed this, citing real-world experience and multiple scientific studies to confirm that the United States can safely and reliably operate the electric grid with high levels of renewables.

Many utilities, though, still don't consider the full value of wind, solar, and other renewable sources. Energy planners often consider narrow cost parameters, and miss the big-picture, long-term opportunities that renewables offer. Increased awareness—and a willingness to move beyond the reliability myth—is sorely needed.

Germany's Energy Transition Stirs Controversy

Sören Amelang

Sören Amelang is a staff correspondent for the Clean Energy Wire. *He spent fifteen years at Reuters, where he wrote about international business, economics, and politics. The* Clean Energy Wire *provides news and background on German energy and policy.*

T he German Renewable Energy Act (EEG) is the mechanism that has made possible the energy transition so far. It guaranteed renewable energy producers high returns on investment, which in turn helped to bring down the costs of installing renewable power capacity. Lawmakers now say the sector is mature enough to take the training wheels off and be exposed to market forces. Major reform of the EEG aims to do just that, reducing costs for consumers. At the same time, the new legislation will limit how much new renewable capacity can be built each year. But the plans are hugely controversial. Big energy companies and industry see it as a step in the right direction. The renewable lobby and citizens' energy groups say it will result in Germany missing its climate targets and betray the collective spirit of the Energiewende in an effort to appease big business.

A Controversial Reform

Renewable companies sending employees out to demonstrate, Twitter campaigns, protest advertisements, and repeated late-night negotiations at Angela Merkel's chancellery—rarely has a rather technical energy policy reform caused such a storm. But Germany's overhaul of the core law behind the country's shift to renewables has touched a nerve.

"The reform is Germany's first fall of man since the Paris Climate Agreement," says Greenpeace energy expert Tobias Austrup.

Patrick Graichen, head of energy think tank Agora Energiewende, begs to differ: "It's the logical next step for renewables."

The controversial reform will expose the renewable power sector to market forces, and at the same time set strict caps on its growth for the first time. In effect, it will slow down the rate of renewable expansion seen in 2014 and 2015. Environmentalists are alarmed. They say the changes will put Germany's climate targets beyond reach, and sound a death knell for citizen-owned energy, so far a fundamental part of Germany's shift to green power. The renewable sector, which employs hundreds of thousands of people in Germany, fears that "putting the breaks on the energy transition" will put many jobs at risk.

Rapid Growth of Renewables

On the rare spring and summer days when bright sunshine comes with strong winds, pushing renewable power production to a peak, Germany can almost cover its entire electricity demand with green power, at least for a few hours at a time. Over the year, the world's fourth largest industrial nation now covers around a third of its total electricity needs with renewables.

This achievement has been possible thanks to Germany's financial support system for green power, enshrined in the so-called Renewable Energy Act (EEG). This law is about to undergo the most profound changes since its inception a quarter of a century ago. With Germany's energy transition—or Energiewende—so far largely limited to the power sector, the country is in effect revamping the cornerstone of the project.

What Is the Renewable Energy Act?

Under the Renewable Energy Act, which has been imitated around the world, any renewable power investor—be it a household installing a solar array on the roof, a cooperative erecting a windmill, a farmer running a biogas installation, or an institutional investor operating an offshore wind park—could sell their green electricity at a guaranteed price above wholesale market price, fixed in advance for 20 years.

These so-called "feed-in tariffs" for green energy spurred a huge wave of renewable energy projects in Germany by offering safe returns on investment. Growing demand meant the cost of renewable installations fell fast and the fixed tariffs offered lucrative returns. As a result, Germany now boasts more than 1.5 million renewable power facilities. The share of renewables in the country's electricity generation rose from 3.6 percent in 1990, when the law was enacted, to 30 percent in 2015.

But critics point out that costs have also shot up. With more and more green power fed onto the grid at above-market prices, the bill has got bigger and bigger. The difference between the feed-in tariffs and the (mostly falling) market price is passed on to consumers in the form of a surcharge added to their power bills. In 2015, consumers paid more than 20 billion euros to green energy producers through these surcharges. On top of this, integrating all that fluctuating renewable power into the existing grid has become increasingly complicated, resulting in further costs. Household power prices have gone up, prompting calls to put a cap on development. In addition, the EU said it favoured the introduction of market-based mechanism for renewable support— But opinions differ on whether this was an important factor for the reform.

A New Era for Renewables

The government first decided to address these issues by reforming the Renewable Energy Act in 2014. Now, there's a draft on the table spelling out how the new rules will work. To get a better grip on renewables development and keep costs under control, feed-in tariffs are to be replaced with a competitive auction system from the start of 2017. First, the government will announce how much new renewable capacity is to be built. Investors then offer a price at which they are prepared to sell electricity from their planned projects. Installations offerings the cheapest electricity win the auction—and are guaranteed that price for the following 20 years.

The basic idea behind this change is that the government will have the power to steer the sector's growth and avoid overshooting the target range of 40-45 percent of power consumed in 2025 coming from renewables. The government also says the reforms ensure only the most economically efficient projects will be realised, thus lowering total costs.

Energy minister Sigmar Gabriel calls the reform a "paradigm shift" and insists the pending changes reflect the fact that renewables in Germany have matured and can no longer claim the "fledgling status" that required feed-in tariffs to shelter them from market forces. The ministry says the reforms—which contain many other changes alongside the auction system and are dubbed EEG 3.0— will future-proof the system, allowing the Energiewende's focus to shift to other major challenges, such as decarbonising the transport and heating sectors.

There is much agreement that a profound shift is on the horizon for Germany's energy transition. The Süddeutsche Zeitung called the reform a "new era for renewables." But opinions vary widely on how the reformed legislation will affect Germany's closely watched move towards a nuclear-free and low-carbon future energy supply. Above all, three issues are at stake: Will it lower the costs of the energy transition? Does the reform endanger Germany's climate targets? And will it kill off citizens' participation in the Energiewende?

Will the Reform Lower Costs?

The government says it is necessary to limit renewable development to allow lagging grid development to keep pace with rising green power generation, and that auctions will ensure only the cheapest projects are realised.

Graichen of Agora Energiewende says the revised law will broadly achieve these targets. "The reforms are the next logical step for renewables. You can't stick to feed-in tariffs agreed by the Bundestag if renewables are the largest player in the power market."

The government began trial auctions for large-scale photovoltaic arrays in 2015. It says high participation and falling prices at each round prove their success. But critics warn that the system does not guarantee how many winning projects will be realised.

The new auctions are to cover more than 80 percent of new renewable energy capacity—only small to medium photovoltaic arrays (with a capacity of up to 750 kilowatts—an installation covering roughly three football (soccer) pitches) will remain exempt from the process. The government says it wants to focus funding on wind and solar, because these technologies contribute most to attaining expansion targets from EEG 2014, whereas hydropower, biomass and geothermal do not offer much potential for growth.

Proponents of the strict limit on renewable development inherent in the auction system argue that the power grid is already stretched to its limits and cannot absorb more wind energy without expensive upgrades. The leader of the conservative CDU parliamentary group, Volker Kauder, called for a general adaptation of renewable development to grid extensions in order to lower costs. He also said new installations should no longer receive compensation if they have to be switched off at times of grid overload.

But energy policy expert Claudia Kemfert at the German Institute for Economic Research (DIW) says the reforms will be a double failure. She argues that auctions will not lower costs, and will fall short of meeting growth corridors. "Auctions reduce planning security and increase financial risks for investors. The corresponding risk premium increases the cost of the Energiewende. Additionally, growth corridors will be missed, if companies win an auction but postpone construction for whatever reason."

Volker Breisig, partner utilities and regulation at pwc advisory, told the Clean Energy Wire it also remained uncertain whether enough investors will participate at the demanding wind tenders. "Especially the rising complexity and an increase in risk could slow development [...] My feeling is that auctions will lower costs, but we have no idea yet how high the risk premium will be," says Breisig, who advises past and new energy suppliers and energy users.

Kemfert, in contrast to most other experts, also says that the success of the Energiewende does not depend on grid extensions. "Our studies and models show that grid extension does no harm, but it's not strictly necessary [...] decentralised, intelligent grids with demand management, and—in the medium term—storage, would be much more important."

Kemfert argues that an oversupply of "yesterday's coal power" rather than tomorrow's renewables is the reason grid extensions are needed. A recent Greenpeace study came to similar conclusions—that power from conventional power plants is blocking the grid, not renewable power. Greenpeace energy expert Austrup says the government aim to synchronise the renewable rollout with grid extensions is "nonsense and only an excuse to put a break on renewables." He adds: "Even at peak renewable production, nuclear power stations continue to run on full steam. The real aim should be to get rid of inflexible power stations."

Graichen says that on a regional basis, these criticisms may be justified because many fossil and nuclear power plants are too inflexible to stop generation at times of peak renewable production.

Advocates of faster renewable development also argue breaks on the green power rollout will do little to reduce costs. In a study for the environment ministry of the German state of Baden-Württemberg, the Institute for Applied Ecology calculated that limiting renewable development will only have a marginal impact on power prices for consumers. This is because the bulk of the cost is for early renewables installations, which still receive high feed-in tariffs set up to 20 years ago. In contrast, new installations are paid a much lower rate and therefore have a smaller impact on costs.

According to Agora Energiewende, the renewable surcharge will likely peak in 2023 and decline thereafter. "The main reason for the foreseeable decline in the EEG surcharge is that from 2023 on, expensive facilities built in the early years of the EEG will lose their claim to a subsidy, while new facilities are already producing power very cost-effectively and will continue to become even cheaper," according to Patrick Graichen.

Climate Targets in Danger?

The reform sets out growth corridors for renewables, which were first agreed in 2014. New wind capacity has been installed so rapidly in the last few years, it looked increasingly likely that Germany would overshoot its target of 40-45 percent of total power consumption coming from renewables by 2025. The aim is to increase that share to 55-60 percent by 2035 and to at least 80 percent by 2050.

To achieve these targets, the reform stipulates "deployment corridors" for different renewable technologies. Each year, 2.5 gigawatts (GW) of photovoltaic capacity is to be installed, of which 600 megawatts (MW) will be auctioned. Onshore wind installations will be set at 2.8 GW per year from 2017 to 2019 and at 2.9 GW from 2020 on - equivalent to around 1,000 new wind turbines per year. The country's total offshore wind capacity is to reach 6.5 GW by 2020 and 15 GW by 2030, by auctioning 730 MW per year. Biomass capacity is to be expanded by 150 megawatts (MW) annually over the next three years and by 200 MW in the following three years.

Environmental organisations and renewable proponents say this rate of growth is far too low to achieve Germany's climate targets.

"To reduce renewables to 45 percent in 2025 means expanding the fossil [fuel] share to 55 percent, with the aim of mitigating the impact on large utilities," Greenpeace energy expert Austrup told the Clean Energy Wire. "What is more important, securing the survival of large companies, or international climate protection?"

A study by the University of Applied Sciences Berlin (HTW) concludes that Germany needs to step up renewable development four- to five times to reach the Paris climate targets, which require the total decarbonisation of the energy sector by 2040. With electricity demand set to rise due to the pending electrification of the transport and heating sectors, the new deployment targets mean

Germany will fall well short of its renewable targets, according to the study. Its author, Volker Quaschning, professor of regenerative energy systems at HTW, says onshore wind power must grow by 6.3 GW net each year, rather than the planned 2.8 GW; solar PV would have to grow by 15 GW instead of 2.5 GW.

Kemfert agrees. "Electric mobility only makes sense when you use renewable energy. This is exactly why we should push renewable development instead of slowing it down."

The government is aware that electrifying transport and heating might push up power demand significantly in the future. But state secretary for energy Rainer Baake said at a conference earlier this year the renewable target corridors could imply much more green electricity than some critics assume, because they specify percentages, rather than absolute volumes. He also said that the auction system would allow steering up renewable capacities in that direction if necessary. "If the demand for electricity rises, we will get the necessary majority for higher auction volumes," Baake said. "But it doesn't make sense to generate more electricity now, without a corresponding demand."

Patrick Graichen of Agora Energiewende says that in the long term, deployment corridors set out in the reform proposal are too low. "The renewable targets for 2025 will surely be achieved with the deployment corridors. The reform aims to prevent a significant overshooting. But the amounts will not be sufficient by a long shot to reach the longer-term renewable targets."

Still, energy minister Gabriel argues that containing costs is crucial to securing the Energiewende's real environmental impact. He says Germany's share in global emissions is so small that the Energiewende can't prevent global warming by itself, but only by being adopted around the world. Therefore, Germany must prove it can manage the transition to renewables without too much damage to its industry. "Otherwise, no other country will follow our lead," Gabriel said at a conference in spring 2016.

German industry association BDI echoed the feelings of many traditional manufacturers worried about rising power costs when it said the reforms were "steps long overdue [...] Up until now, renewable energies in Germany were driven forward regardless of costs, supply security and grid development."

The End of Citizens' Energy Cooperatives?

A third question is over citizens' participation in the Energiewende. It's estimated that in 2012, nearly half of Germany's renewable energy capacity was owned by citizens through private installations and energy cooperatives. The economics and energy ministry says "ensuring a high level of diversity," including small cooperatives, is one of three core objectives of the auction process, the others being the ability to plan the energy transition and to keep costs down by introducing competition. But critics say the new rules give corporate projects an unfair advantage over cooperative ones.

"We expect the new rules will spell the end of new cooperative projects," Andreas Wieg, head of the National Office for Energy Cooperatives told Clean Energy Wire. "Auctions are problematic for typical citizen cooperatives, because they involve very high upfront costs of 50,000 to 100,000 euros. If they don't win the auction, that money is lost."

Wieg says cooperatives typically only plan to realise a single project and cannot therefore split the risk of loosing an auction—in contrast to large commercial project developers who can participate with several projects at once.

In the wake of such criticism, the ministry published an additional concept on how to facilitate the participation of citizen cooperatives in wind energy auctions, by exempting them from certain regulatory requirements. But Kemfert calls the concept a "desperate attempt" to remedy the situation: "Citizen's energy cooperatives are the big losers of this reform."

After he tabled the proposal, Baake told a citizens' energy audience it was his ministry's firm intention to preserve the variety of actors that is a "trademark of the German energy transition." He said the successful participation of cooperatives in pilot solar tenders was proof that citizens' energy projects can compete successfully at auctions.

But Wieg says the winning bids by cooperatives were older projects planned under the old EEG rules that weren't finished on time.

Greenpeace's Austrup says the new rules will change the character of the energy transition, by dramatically reducing the number of players: "The Energiewende turns into a project of large companies. Crowding out local initiatives spells trouble for the acceptance of the energy transition."

Many representatives of the renewable industry say the reform is a thinly veiled attempt to secure the survival of large utilities mainly focused on conventional power stations—namely E.ON, RWE, EnBW and Vattenfall. Chancellor Angela Merkel stressed at a utility conference in June 2016 that the Energiewende must not push utilities over the brink, saying "we have to make sure the basic providers of energy do not collapse under the burdens caused by the Energiewende."

Breisig from pwc advisory says the complexity of the tender system will generally favour large companies. "It is definitely a professionalization of renewable development."

In opinion polls, a large majority of Germans say they are in favour of the energy transition. But many experts say citizen participation is crucial to maintaining public support for renewables and overcoming local opposition to specific renewable projects such as wind farms.

"Direct citizen participation is the only way to solve the problem of acceptance, or the not-in-my-backyard mentality," insists Wieg. "Even if energy cooperatives have only contributed a fraction of total renewable capacity, they represent 160,000 people. To gather the motivation for future challenges of the energy transition—such as efficiency, smart grids, a transition in mobility, among others—we need to have a large section of the populace on board."

Large commercial investors on the other hand have applauded the transition to auctions. E.ON spokesperson Markus Nitschke told the Clean Energy Wire. "We broadly agree with the intention of the energy and economics ministry to move towards greater competition." Danish offshore wind power company Dong Energy has also welcomed the reform plans, arguing that auctions would help reduce prices and increase competition.

One possibility to secure a role for cooperatives in the future might be participation in large commercial projects. E.ON's Nitschke told the Clean Energy Wire: "It has become our standard procedure to offer local residents involvement in onshore wind projects. It's a question of acceptance."

Wieg welcomes E.ON's approach, but says citizens must be able to do more than just invest their money. "Is it just about a little financial stake, or are they really allowed to play along? A true feeling of local ownership is crucial. Depending on the specific realisation, the impact on acceptance and motivation is very different."

Breisig says the reforms will force investors of many types into alliances: "This will be something entirely new."

Current
CONTROVERSIES

CHAPTER 3

Does Clean Energy Work?

Possible Scenarios in the Future of Energy

World Energy Council

The World Energy Council is an impartial network of organizations dedicated to the promotion of affordable, stable, and environmentally sensitive energy systems for the benefit of all peoples.

Scenarios are alternative views of the future which can be used to explore the implications of different sets of assumptions and to determine the degree of robustness of possible future developments. While most widely known scenarios are normative, the WEC has adopted a different, exploratory approach. "Normative" in this context means that the scenarios are being used to drive the world towards a specific objective such as a particular atmospheric CO_2 level. In contrast, the WEC with its exploratory scenarios Jazz and Symphony, attempts to provide decision makers with a neutral fact-based tool that they will be able to use to measure the potential impact of their choices in the future.

Rather than telling policymakers and senior energy leaders what to do, in order to achieve a specific policy goal, the WEC's World Energy Scenarios to 2050 will allow them to test the key assumptions that they decide to make to shape the energy of tomorrow. Investors can use this tool to assess which are likely to be the most dynamic areas and real game-changers of tomorrow.

These scenarios are therefore likely to change the way energy decision makers consider the choices they make in understanding the real impact of their actions in the long term.

This approach can only be done successfully by a network like the WEC's with its impartial and inclusive membership structure. Over 60 experts from more than 28 countries have contributed

"World Energy Scenarios: Composing energy futures to 2050," World Energy Council, September 2013. Reprinted by permission.

to the WEC's scenario building process over a period of three years.

Assessing the Energy Trilemma

These scenarios are designed to help a range of stakeholders address the "energy trilemma" of achieving environmental sustainability, energy security, and energy equity and hence putting forward different policy options.

Clearly, each policy option has some cost associated with it. The cost of one scenario versus the other must not only be considered in terms of necessary capital investments and the impact on and of gross domestic product (GDP) growth; the overall environmental benefits and avoided climate change adaptation costs also need to be taken into account. This means that one scenario is not necessarily better than the other and should not be judged as such. Instead, a wider view needs to be adopted when assessing the overall implications of each of the scenarios.

World Energy Scenarios 10 Key Messages

1. Energy system complexity will increase by 2050.
2. Energy efficiency is crucial in dealing with demand outstripping supply.
3. The energy mix in 2050 will mainly be fossil based.
4. Regional priorities differ: there is no "one-size-fits-all" solution to the energy trilemma.
5. The global economy will be challenged to meet the 450ppm target without unacceptable carbon prices.
6. A low-carbon future is not only linked to renewables: carbon capture, utilisation and storage (CC(U)S) is important and consumer behaviour needs changing.
7. CC(U)S technology, solar energy and energy storage are the key uncertainties up to 2050.
8. Balancing the energy trilemma means making difficult choices.

9. Functioning energy markets require investments and regional integration to deliver benefits to all consumers.
10. Energy policy should ensure that energy and carbon markets deliver.

Composing Energy Futures to 2050

The WEC has built two scenarios typified by characteristics, which, each from their own perspective, may comprehensively describe large parts of the world in 2050. In this scenario exercise, the elements of the two scenarios are generalised as being applicable to the (albeit imaginary) whole world: the more consumer- driven Jazz scenario and the more voter-driven Symphony scenario. While the scenarios are 'music based', they are completely different in nature.

Jazz

As an energy scenario, Jazz has a focus on energy equity with priority given to achieving individual access and affordability of energy through economic growth.

Jazz is a style of music, characterised by a strong but flexible rhythmic structure with solo and ensemble improvisations on basic tunes and chord patterns. In Jazz, musicians have freedom to take the lead and improvise; others in the band will often follow.

Symphony

As an energy scenario, Symphony has a focus on achieving environmental sustainability through internationally coordinated policies and practices.

A Symphony is a complex piece of music with a fixed structure composed to be played by a symphony orchestra. The orchestra will have a conductor and 80 or so orchestra members will each have a specific role to play and score to follow.

The WEC's Scenarios Findings: Composing Energy Futures

Energy Landscape in 2050

The energy landscape we expect to see in 2050 will be quite different from how it looks today. Meeting future energy demand will be a key challenge. The world's population will increase from approximately 7 billion in 2013 to approximately 8.7 billion in the Jazz scenario and approximately 9.4 billion in the Symphony scenario in 2050, which is equal to a 26% increase (36% respectively). The GDP per capita will also increase from slightly more than 9,000 US$2010 on average globally (US$2010 MER) in 2010 to approximately 23,000 US$2010 in Jazz and about 18,000 US$2010 in Symphony in 2050. This represents an increase by 153% and 100%, respectively. Mobility will also increase, with car ownership in terms of cars per 1,000 people increasing from 124 in 2010 to 244 in 2050 in Jazz and 193 in Symphony. This equates to an increase by 98% and 57% respectively.

What Jazz and Symphony Can Offer

Many key messages arise from the Jazz and Symphony scenarios. One of these is that more international cooperation, including internationally harmonised politics and trust in market mechanisms, is essential for achieving environmental goals, energy security and energy equity. Jazz and Symphony can contribute towards enhancing the debate on how these goals can best be achieved, taking into account a wide range of policy options. The WEC's World Energy Scenarios to 2050 will help strengthen the debate on how collaboration among all relevant stakeholders in the energy field can effectively be implemented.

Energy System Complexity Will Increase by 2050

The WEC estimates that total primary energy supply (equal to consumption) will increase globally from 546 EJ (152 PWh) in 2010 to 879 EJ (144 PWh) in the Jazz scenario and 696 EJ (193 PWh) in the Symphony scenario in 2050. This corresponds to an increase of 61% in Jazz and 27% in Symphony. Just to compare: from 1990 to 2010—which is roughly half the time span covered in this scenario study—total global primary energy consumption rose by approximately 45%. It is expected that global primary energy consumption will continue to rise, but at a much lower rate than in previous decades. Meeting both global and regional energy demand will be a challenge. There is no one global solution to the energy supply issue. Instead, each of the individual parts of the challenge must be worked out to reach the global goal of sustainable, affordable and secure energy supply for all.

Energy Efficiency Is Crucial in Dealing with Demand Outstripping Supply

Energy efficiency will increase significantly in both scenarios: primary energy intensity as measured in energy use per unit of GDP created will decrease by 50% and 53% in Jazz and Symphony respectively by 2050. Hence when comparing primary energy consumption to GDP produced, only half the amount of energy is needed until 2050 to produce the same output. This is true for both scenarios although primary energy consumption is higher in 2050 in the Jazz scenario than it is in the Symphony scenario. WEC World Energy Scenarios to 2050 show that energy efficiency and energy conservation are absolutely crucial in dealing with demand outstripping supply—both require a change in consumer priorities and have cost implications across industries—and hence capital is required to finance energy- efficiency measures in terms of an initial investment before it can pay off.

The Energy Mix in 2050 Will Mainly Be Fossil Fuel Based

The future primary energy mix in 2050 shows that growth rates will be highest for renewable energy sources. In absolute terms, fossil fuels (coal, oil, gas) will remain dominant, up to and including

2050. The share of fossil fuels will be 77% in the Jazz scenario and 59% in the Symphony scenario—compared to 79% in 2010. The share of renewable energy sources will increase from around 15% in 2010 to almost 20% in Jazz in 2050 and almost 30% in Symphony in 2050. Nuclear energy will contribute approximately 4% of total primary energy supply in Jazz in 2050 and 11% in Symphony globally—compared to 6% in 2010.

Global Electricity Generation Will Increase Between 123% and 150% by 2050

Global electricity generation will increase between now and 2050: In 2010, global electricity production was 21.5 billion MWh globally. In Jazz, this is expected to increase by 150% to 53.6 billion MWh by 2050. In Symphony, the increase is about 123% to 47.9 billion MWh by 2050. Simply due to the sheer increase in electricity production that is needed to meet future demand, the future electricity generation mix will be subject to tremendous changes up to 2050.

Investment Needs in Electricity Generation Will Be Between $19 Trillion and $26 Trillion Worldwide in 2050

Huge investment in electricity generation is needed to meet future electricity demand. The WEC estimates that total investment needed will range from US$19 trillion in Jazz to US$26 trillion in Symphony (in 2010 terms)—in terms of cumulative investment in electricity generation in both scenarios (2010–2050, undiscounted). Depending on each scenario, a share of 46% in Jazz and almost 70% in Symphony of this is to be invested in renewable electricity generation. Major investment requirements are in solar PV, hydro and wind electricity generation capacity. The WEC's work clearly highlights that the availability of funds for investment is one of the key clusters in scenario building terms that will shape the energy landscape until 2050.

The Overall Degree of Energy Access Will Increase. Africa Faces Great Challenges to Increase Access to Electricity

The degree of electrification measured in terms of the share of electric energy on the final energy mix, increases up to 2050 significantly. In Jazz, the degree of electrification will be almost 30% in 2050, in Symphony this will even be slightly more than 30% in 2050—as compared to 17% in 2010.

Electricity consumption per capita increases globally by 111% in Jazz and 78% in Symphony in 2050.

Electricity access, measured as the share of population connected to the electricity grid will increase in both scenarios: energy access will hence improve. While in 2010, 1.267 billion people were without access to electricity globally, this reduces to 319 million in Jazz and 530 million in the Symphony scenario in 2050.

Regional Priorities Differ: There Is No "One-Size-Fits-All" Solution to the Energy Trilemma

Future economic growth shifts from developed countries to developing and transition economies, in particular in Asia. Of all the eight regions considered in this scenario study, Asia will be characterised by highest economic growth both in relative and absolute terms. By 2050, nearly half of all economic growth (measured in terms of production of GDP) will happen in Asia and its three sub-regions: Central and South Asia, East Asia and Southeast Asia and Pacific both for Jazz and Symphony. This means that the share of Asia on total primary energy consumption will increase from 40% in 2010 to 48% in Jazz and 45% in Symphony. To compare: by 2050, Europe and North America (including Mexico) will make up for about 30% of total global primary energy consumption in Jazz and 31% in Symphony (2010: 44%). Africa, including the Middle East will account for 15% (Jazz) and 16% in Symphony (2010: 11%) and Latin America and The Caribbean 8% in Jazz and 7% in Symphony (2010: 5%).

The Global Economy Will Be Challenged to Meet the 450ppm Target Without Unacceptable Carbon Prices

The WEC has analysed where the Jazz and Symphony scenarios might lead in terms of climate change. The WEC has also assessed the potential impact of Jazz and Symphony scenarios on the climate with reference to the work of the Intergovernmental Panel on Climate Change (IPCC).

Jazz Scenario

In Jazz, an assumption is made that the negotiations on climate change and emissions targets are not finalised. In the absence of international agreed commitments, regions, countries, states and municipalities take their own sustainable development initiatives and pathways. An international carbon market grows slowly from the bottom up based on regional, national and local initiatives, which coalesce to achieve greater market efficiencies and liquidity.

Commercially viable innovative low-carbon technologies (solar, wind, and city gas/waste to energy) experience growth, major reductions in CO_2 emissions come from growth in natural gas, in preference to oil and coal for purely economic reasons.

Symphony Scenario

In Symphony, countries pass through the Doha Gateway and successfully negotiate a global treaty because all countries are prepared to accept commitments and concessions. Climate change has more focus along with international initiatives on climate change. Low-carbon technologies are promoted despite lacking commercial viability at initial stages.

The carbon market is top-down based on an international agreement, with commitments and allocations. In the early part of the scenario period, national initiatives to meet treaty obligations to reduce emissions emerge (developed and developing countries). These national initiatives are linked to form regional markets with exchange of Clean Development Mechanism

(CDM) and other emission units. The final part of the scenario period sees global action on climate change with the market instrument emission trading as the leading mechanism for meeting CO_2 emission obligations.

The WEC's Commitment to Climate Change

At the COP 15 (Conference of Parties) meeting, the 15th session of the United Nations (UN) Framework Convention on Climate Change, the "Copenhagen Agreement" or "Copenhagen Accord" was ratified by delegates and they endorsed the continuation of the Kyoto Protocol. Specific emissions-reduction targets for 2020 were submitted by individual countries. At subsequent COP meetings, this was reinforced, in particular at the COP18 meeting in Doha when the "Doha Climate Gateway" was developed—a package of deals that set out a work programme through which both rich and developing countries can deliver a new international climate agreement. The Doha Climate Gateway includes a timetable for a 2015 global climate change agreement and for increasing ambitions before 2020. At Doha, countries agreed a course for negotiating the Durban Platform for Enhanced Action, a new climate deal for all countries to be agreed by 2015 and to take effect in 2020—the Ad Hoc Working Group on the Durban Platform for Enhanced Action (ADP).

To establish a clear link between energy use and climate change objectives, the WEC has included the Doha Climate Gateway as a key differentiator between its two scenarios. The WEC assumes that in the Symphony scenario, countries pass through the Gateway and successfully negotiate a global treaty. In the Jazz scenario, these negotiations fail, and regions, countries, states and municipalities take their own sustainable development pathways.

The WEC's Scenarios and Climate Implications

Although Jazz includes a stronger emphasis on adaptation and Symphony mitigation, in both scenarios additional action is expected over the longer term (beyond 2050), further reducing the impact on climate. The implications of these changes to atmospheric GHG concentrations for surface temperature change, sea-level rise, changes in precipitation, incidence of extreme events and other impacts remain uncertain.

Pressure for climate action will change over the period, the WEC recognises that the climate forcing of CO_2 is considered now to be lower in some of the scientific literature in 2013. There is also increasing awareness of severe weather events that could be linked to climate forcing.

A Low-Carbon Future Is Not Only Linked to Renewables: CC(U)S Is Important and Consumer Behaviour Needs Changing

CO_2 emissions will increase in both scenarios in the first half of the scenario period. In the Symphony scenario, where, by assumption, greater emphasis is placed on climate change mitigation and adaptation, a turning point will be reached by 2020. In the Jazz scenario, the turning point is only reached by 2040. As far as the total amount of CO_2 emissions are concerned, both scenarios differ substantially. In the Jazz scenario, CO_2 emissions will be more than 44 billion tonnes per annum in 2050 which is 45% higher than in 2010. In the Symphony scenario, CO_2 emissions reach 19 billion tonnes per annum which is nearly 40% lower than in 2010. The WEC's World Energy Scenarios to 2050 underline that a reduction of greenhouse gas emissions is possible in the second half of the scenario period with global agreements and the implementation of cost-efficient measures like emissions trading within a cap and trade system (assumed in Symphony).

Toward Low-Carbon Electricity Generation

Electricity generation from renewable energy sources (RES-E) will increase around four to five times by 2050 in comparison to 2010. This is strongest in the Symphony scenario. In Symphony, electricity generation from hydro doubles, for biomass the increase is eight-fold, and for wind eleven-fold when comparing figures for 2010 with 2050. Solar PV has the highest increase of approximately

230 times between 2010 and 2050. By 2050, globally, almost as much electricity is produced from solar PV as from coal (coal and coal with CC(U)S).

The share of renewable energy sources for electricity generation will increase from approximately 20% in 2010 to more than 30% in 2050 in Jazz and nearly 50% in Symphony.

The degree to which renewable energy sources will be used and investment in CC(U)S technologies for coal and gas (and also biomass) will be decisive in mitigating climate change.

CC(U)S Technology, Solar Energy and Energy Storage Are the Key Uncertainties Up to 2050

Carbon capture utilisation and storage (CC(U)S) technologies are widely employed in Symphony and hence subject to higher growth rates in the Symphony scenario than in the Jazz scenario. Half of the total electricity generated based on fossil fuels will be in conjunction with CC(U)S in 2050 in Symphony. Combining nuclear and CC(U)S for gas, coal and biomass, more than 80% of all electricity generated in 2050 will be from low-carbon sources in the Symphony scenario, compared to 40% in the Jazz scenario. To compare: In 2010, only one-third of global electricity generation was CO_2 from low-carbon sources.

The WEC believes that CC(U)S technology, solar energy and energy storage are the key uncertainties moving forward up to 2050. For CC(U)S to work, clear legislative frameworks are needed— combined with infrastructure investment and the right incentives. A low-carbon future is not only linked to renewables: CC(U)S is important and consumer behaviour needs changing. Changes in consumption habits can be an effective way to decarbonise the energy system. Voters need to balance local and global issues.

Assessment of Jazz vs. Symphony

The WEC believes that a balanced trilemma can only be achieved through compromises and global initiatives. Together with energy efficiency, CC(U)S, solar and wind will be the key technologies driving change forward.

Jazz

- On average, energy equity progresses better
- More people are able to afford more energy because the global market leads to higher GDP growth
- Emissions don't drop until after 2040
- Performance improves markedly if a bottom-up carbon market develops early in the scenario, but the higher GDP growth still means higher emissions
- Puts more emphasis on adaptation

Symphony

- Energy equity is less because there are inevitably interventions restricting GDP growth
- Funds directed into low-carbon initiatives would actually start diverting funds from other government priorities such as health care and other programmes
- Financial resources are not limitless
- Governments have to set spending priorities
- Scores well on environmental impact mitigation particularly CO_2 emission reduction, with emissions dropping after 2020
- Externalities are more effectively internalised: this is primarily because countries adopt a range of mechanisms to meet treaty obligations on CO_2
- Higher carbon prices would achieve higher emission reduction
- The market instrument emission trading is assumed as the leading mechanism for meeting CO_2 emission obligations in the second part of the scenario period

[…]

Renewable Energy Can Provide Most of the United States' Electricity

Union of Concerned Scientists

The Union of Concerned Scientists develops and implements innovative and practical solutions to the planet's most pressing problems, including global warming, finding sustainable methods of food development and transport, and reducing the threat of nuclear war.

A comprehensive study by the Department of Energy's National Renewable Energy Laboratory (NREL) shows that the US can generate most of its electricity from renewable energy by 2050.

The Renewable Electricity Futures Study found that an 80 percent renewables future is feasible with currently available technologies, including wind turbines, solar photovoltaics, concentrating solar power, biopower, geothermal, and hydropower.

The study also demonstrates that a high renewables scenario can meet electricity demand across the country every hour of every day, year-round.

Variable resources such as wind and solar power can provide up to about half of US electricity, with the remaining 30 percent from other renewable sources.

Increasing renewables to supply 80 percent of US electricity does not, however, limit energy choices to one specific pathway. Rather, the NREL study shows that a range of renewable energy scenarios provide the nation with multiple pathways to reach this goal.

Ramping Up Renewable Energy Provides Significant Benefits...

Renewable energy provides substantial benefits for our climate, our health, and our economy. It dramatically reduces global warming emissions, improves public health, and provides jobs and other economic benefits. And since most renewables don't require water for cooling, they dramatically reduce the water requirements for power production compared to fossil-fueled power plants.

In an 80 percent renewables future, carbon emissions from the power sector would be reduced by 80 percent, and water use would be reduced by 50 percent.

...But We Need the Right Policies to Make It Happen

The NREL study makes it clear that the 80 percent renewables future is technically feasible and affordable, but can only be achieved with the right policies and measures in place.

We already have the tools to start significantly ramping up renewable energy today. But we must also work to improve the electricity grid with increased transmission infrastructure to integrate a high amount of renewable generation, and incorporate more advanced grid planning to maintain reliability.

Ultimately, the US needs a long-term clean energy policy that create a long-term market for renewable energy, encourages and supports the integration of renewable energy, puts a price on carbon emissions, and increases funding for research and development.

More About the Renewable Electricity Futures Study

The Renewable Electricity Futures Study is arguably the most comprehensive analysis of a high renewable electricity future to date.

The study was assessed by 140 peer reviewers, used state-of-the-art modeling to achieve the results, and includes detailed assessments of costs, challenges, and opportunities for each renewable energy technology. It serves as an accurate, realistic portrayal of what can be achieved in the coming decades.

Since the study was performed at a very fine geographic and time scale (looking at 134 regions across the US on an hourly basis) the results are robust and closely detail how renewable energy sources and potential vary by region.

Some parts of the country have substantial wind resources. Other areas have more solar potential. Still others have extensive biomass or geothermal resources.

The Bright Future of Electricity

World Economic Forum

Based in Cologny, Switzerland, and founded in 1971 by Klaus Schwab, the World Economic Forum is a nonprofit organization committed to improving the state of the world through business, politics, and academic education.

The electricity system is in the midst of a transformation, as technology and innovation disrupt traditional models from generation to beyond the meter. Three trends in particular are converging to produce game-changing disruptions:

- Electrification of large sectors of the economy such as transport and heating
- Decentralization, spurred by the sharp decrease in costs of distributed energy resources (DERs) like distributed storage, distributed generation, demand flexibility and energy efficiency
- Digitalization of both the grid, with smart metering, smart sensors, automation and other digital network technologies, and beyond the meter, with the advent of the Internet of Things (IoT) and a surge of power-consuming connected devices

These three trends act in a virtuous cycle, enabling, amplifying and reinforcing developments beyond their individual contributions. Electrification is critical for long-term carbon reduction goals and will represent an increasingly relevant share of renewable energy. Decentralization makes customers active elements of the system and requires significant coordination. Digitalization supports both the other trends by enabling more control, including automatic, real-time optimization of consumption and production and interaction with customers.

"The Future of Electricity: New Technologies Transforming the Grid Edge," World Economic Forum, March 2017. Reprinted by permission.

Three factors fuel the potential for disruption by these grid edge technologies:

1. Their exponentially decreasing costs and continuous technical enhancements
2. Their enabling role for innovative business models, built around empowered customers
3. The sizeable improvement to the asset utilization rate of the electricity system, which is typically below 60% in the United States; electric vehicles alone could add several percentage points to system asset utilization (as noted below)

Together, these grid edge trends pave the way towards a system where traditional boundaries between producers, distributors and customers are blurred, increasing the complexity of system governance. Customer preferences and expectations are shifting towards fewer carbon emissions, greater choice, real-time interaction and sharing, always-on connection, higher transparency, experiences and learning opportunities through services more than products, better reliability and security.

Drawing parallels to the media industry and the internet revolution, it is possible to expect that customers will participate differently from before. The role of the grid is evolving beyond supplying electricity and becoming a platform that also maximizes value of distributed energy resources. Revenue models will see a smaller share of income derived from centrally generated electrons, but could be compensated by revenue from new distribution and retail services. Individual customers will be able to select the technologies of their choice, connect them to the grid and eventually transact with other distributed and centralized resources.

This smarter, more decentralized, yet more connected electricity system could increase reliability, security, environmental sustainability, asset utilization and open new opportunities for services and business.

By increasing the efficiency of the overall system, optimizing capital allocation and creating new services for customers, grid edge technologies can unlock significant economic value for the industry, customers and society. Previous analysis by the World Economic Forum has pointed to more than $2.4 trillion of value from the transformation of electricity over the next 10 years. Society will benefit from a cleaner generation mix, net creation of new jobs related to the deployment of these technologies and a larger choice for consumers. Grid edge technologies can also improve social equity by creating value for low-income segments of population. Under the right regulatory model and targeted innovative business models, low-income households could participate and benefit from the value created by grid edge technologies.

Worldwide, several grid edge regulatory innovations showcase the change taking place, including New York's Reforming Energy Vision initiative, Jeju Island's Carbon Free Island initiative, the UK's RIIO regulation and the European Commission's Energy Winter Package. There is also change in the private sector, with new cross-sectoral partnerships to deliver the enabling infrastructure and company reorganizations to develop new business models.

The adoption rate of these grid edge technologies is likely to follow the typical S-curve seen with previous technologies such as TVs, white good appliances and the internet. It has always been difficult to accurately forecast when technologies reach their tipping point and spread at an exponential pace. However, in the past few decades the time to reach the point of mass adoption has decreased to about 15 to 20 years.

It is worth noting that the system faces a great risk of value destruction if it fails to capture the benefits of distributed energy resources, which could result in stranded network assets and eventually customer defection from the grid. This risk represents one more reason to identify and take the most effective action to accelerate the transition and make it cost-effective. The Forum believes this transformation is inevitable and that status quo is not an option. The key issues are, therefore, how the public and private sectors can successfully deal with it and shape it.

An efficient transition towards this new electricity system faces four main challenges. First, electricity is still largely perceived only as a commodity, making customer engagement in new technologies a costly and difficult endeavour. Second, the current regulatory paradigm hinders distributed resources from providing their full value to the system. Third, uncertainty around rules prevents key stakeholders from deploying enabling infrastructure that could complement the grid as the backbone of the future electricity system. Finally, some segments resist a cultural change towards a different allocation of roles and new business models.

The Forum's recommendations, formed after assessing practical examples and best practices in mature markets, fall into four categories:

1. Redesign the regulatory paradigm. Change the rules of the game, advancing and reforming regulation to enable new roles for distribution network operators, innovation and full integration of distributed energy resources

2. Deploy enabling infrastructure. Ensure timely deployment of the infrastructure to enable new business models and the future energy system

3. Redefine customer experience. Incorporate the new reality of a digital, customer-empowered, interactive electricity system

4. Embrace new business models. Pursue new revenue sources from innovative distribution and retail services, and develop business models to adapt to the Fourth Industrial Revolution

Grid edge technologies offer the potential for an exciting transformation of the electricity industry, one that creates more choice for customers, greater efficiency, more efficient decarbonization, and better economics for stakeholders across the value chain. By following the recommendations in this report, policy-makers, regulators and private enterprise can work together to secure the positive changes they offer to electricity markets worldwide.

Grid Edge Challenges and Opportunities

The three technology trends bringing disruption to the electricity industry—electrification, decentralization and digitization – will affect grid and behind-the-meter economics differently depending on their trajectory of adoption. To gain a better understanding of which mechanisms will affect the adoption curve and which tools (including policies and regulations) will accelerate adoption, each of these technology trends is examined in detail below.

Electrification

As generation shifts to more renewable sources, electrification creates further environmental benefits by shifting many end uses of electricity (e.g. transportation and heating) away from fossil fuel sources, and in many cases electrification increases energy efficiency. In OECD markets, the most promising electrification opportunities are in those segments that are among the largest polluters: transportation, commercial/industrial applications and residential heating. In the United States, of the 5 billion tons of CO_2 emissions in 2015, transportation was the largest segment (1.9 billion tons), followed by commercial/industrial processes and manufacturing (1.4 billion tons) and residential heating and appliances (1 billion tons). Light-duty vehicles (cars, small trucks), at 1 billion tons, accounts for slightly more than half (55%) of the transportation segment, making this a critical area for decarbonization and the current focus area for the initiative. Similarly, in the United Kingdom, transport accounts for about 30% of the country's total carbon emissions (422 million tons in 2014), where passenger cars and light-duty vehicles account for the majority of the transport segment.

Electrification of Transport

Electric vehicle (EV) technology has evolved rapidly over the past five years. Range has improved from less than 100 miles (161 km) up to 300 miles (483 km) for some models, addressing a prime convenience issue compared to traditional vehicles with internal-combustion engines (ICEs). The cost of batteries has declined from about $1,000 per kilowatt-hour (kWh) in 2010 to below $300 in 2015, dramatically lowering the cost of EVs and enabling lower-cost models such as the Nissan Leaf or the Tesla Model 3. These price drops have closed the gap with more traditional ICE cars, and buyers can choose from more available models and styles every year. As a result, 2015 was the year where over one million EVs globally were on the road.

Today, electric vehicles in the largest markets benefit from direct subsidies, for example, in the form of tax credits that partially offset higher purchase costs. By 2020, EVs will be economical without subsidies in many countries—reaching three- to five-year breakeven periods compared to an investment in a traditional car or truck. This improvement is due primarily to the declining costs of batteries, which account for most of the cost differential of electric vehicles today. Battery costs are expected to decrease to below $200 per kWh by 2020.

Challenges

Even as EVs are expected to become economically competitive, several infrastructure challenges could limit successful adoption of EVs. First among these is the paucity of charging stations, which lag far behind the number of gasoline stations. Today, slow charging stations cost about $1,200 for a residential charger, $4,000 for a commercial garage charger and $6,000 for a curbside charger. Reallocating EV subsidies from vehicles to charging stations over the next five years could enable the deployment of two to eight times as many charging stations compared to the number of EVs subsidized. Public infrastructure is also lagging behind mostly due to uncertainty related to the model of deployment, including costs, ownership and technical requirements. High-power charging infrastructure (greater than 150kW) positioned along highways would be a good choice for this public infrastructure.

Opportunities

Adoption of EVs will increase electricity consumption, and offer a great opportunity to optimize utilization of the grid. This could be accomplished if recharging technology, together with proper pricing and smart and flexible charging, are deployed—e.g. car owners charge their EVs at times when grid utilization is low (at night) or when supply is very high (windy and sunny afternoons, when renewables are highly productive). In addition, vehicle-to-home/vehicle-to-grid (V2G) technology could be an enabler—where electricity of the batteries can be injected back to the home or grid. In 2015, EVs in California represented about 0.3% of total load, drawing 650 gigawatt hours (GWh). If California reaches its goal of 1.5 million zero-emission vehicles by 2025, they could account for 2% to 3% of the total load in that state, depending on the mix of vehicles. This percentage will continue to climb if EV adoption follows forecast growth. Analysis by the World Economic Forum has shown that this increase in EVs could result in increased system asset utilization by several percentage points.

In broadly cited estimates, in which EV adoption relies on individual customer purchases, EVs will represent a growing and significant portion of new car sales globally: 25% by 2030 and 35% by 2040. Sales at this level would mean that EVs could make up 5% to 10% of total vehicle stock by 2030, in line with International Energy Agency (IEA) estimates to reach the United Nations Framework Convention on Climate Change (UNFCCC) Paris Agreement targets of deploying 100 million electric cars by 2030.

However, under other scenarios, EV adoption could advance even faster. Autonomous driving technology may be one of the biggest accelerators of EV adoption, along with declining battery costs. Electric vehicles also strengthen the economic case for autonomous mobility services such as self-driving taxis, as they offer cost and convenience advantages over conventional vehicles. This technology creates value in several new ways. First, it will allow commuters to focus on working, reading, entertainment or even sleeping rather than driving. Second, autonomous vehicles lend themselves more readily to car sharing when not in use by their owners. This new revenue stream can make the investment in a new car more attractive. A shared car's higher utilization makes a strong case for it to be electric, given their lower operating costs per mile. Ultimately, autonomous technology may encourage a transition to "transportation as a service," where individual customers buy fewer cars and companies own large fleets of electric, autonomous vehicles.

Although the economics of electric vehicles are well suited to fleets of autonomous cars, regulations and laws will have to evolve to allow and encourage these driverless vehicles. Major auto manufacturers project that fully autonomous vehicles will be available in the next 4 to 5 years, especially if fleet companies such as Uber and Lyft invest heavily in the space. If the private sector invests in autonomous technology, EV numbers will probably increase dramatically beyond the projections that rely on individual customer decisions and replacement cycles. This would also have environmental benefits, improving health and air quality in many cities. In addition, the electrification of private and public transportation fleets could further stimulate an introduction of light-duty electric vehicles.

Decentralization

Decentralization refers to several technologies with different implications for the grid:

- Distributed generation from renewable sources (primarily photovoltaic solar) reduces demand during sunny hours of the day.
- Distributed storage collects electrical energy locally for use during peak periods or as backup, flattening demand peaks and valleys.

- Energy efficiency allows for reduced energy use while providing the same service, reducing overall demand.
- Demand response enables control of energy use during peak demand and high pricing periods, reducing peak demand.

Distributed Generation

Incentive programmes to encourage distributed generation in the form of rooftop solar photovoltaic technologies have been extremely effective in many cases, and customers have embraced them in many countries. Deployment of solar PV panels has increased dramatically in recent years with global installed capacity reaching 260 GWp (gigawatt-peak) in 2015 and expected to surpass 700 GWp by 2020. This growth has brought down the installed price of residential solar PV from about $7 per watt in 2009 to $3 per watt in 2015 in the US (and less than $3 in parts of Europe, such as Germany). New technologies, such as rooftop solar tiles and building integrated PV (BIPV), are now becoming available, broadening the future potential of distributed generation.

Challenges

The conventional electricity system regulatory structure was designed around a limited number of large-scale centralized generation assets connected to a grid that carried electricity in one direction, to customers, and divided the one-way flow of power into siloes of various roles across the value chain. With distributed generation, distribution grids become active and see power owing in both directions, with a higher number of active customers to manage and a change in the load profile by reducing demand from the central generation. The requirements that allow management of the flow of electricity in real time, including revised roles of network operators and proper network technology, are yet to be fully developed in most of the countries, along with solid schemes for valuing distributed generation services.

Opportunities

Distributed generation can benefit customers and the system in several valuable ways. For customers, solar can be an attractive and economical option, especially in sunny areas where they generate more electricity. For the system overall and for utilities, distributed generation can supply electricity directly to some percentage of customers, and depending on the status of the grid infrastructure, allows deferral of capital investments to maintain and upgrade grids and related services when these are less economical.

In some cases, distributed generation may be the most affordable and expedient way to support load growth, particularly where it would be too expensive or time consuming or difficult to add new infrastructure. In Southern California, for example, the closure of the San Onofre Nuclear Generating Station and the resulting shortage of centralized capacity created a need for more electricity in a stressed area of the grid in West Los Angeles. As a result, hundreds of megawatts were procured from distributed resources, amounting to about 10% of load capacity requirements. In Hawaii, high land prices and a very mountainous terrain, combined with sunny skies, make distributed generation a pragmatic solution. The technologies can also play a part in rural microgrids, which would be especially important in areas lacking access to electricity.

Distributed Storage

As more renewables come online, the need for storage will become increasingly acute. Without storage, when too much electricity enters the grid on sunny days and windy afternoons or days with reduced demand, supply exceeds demand and negative pricing occurs—as it did more than 7,700 times in California in 2015. Forecasts estimate this imbalance will grow over the next few years as more electricity enters the grid from renewable sources, intensifying the "load duck curve." Storage adds flexibility to the system, allowing those electrons to be stored and discharged later when they are needed—for example in evening hours or during times of peak demand. Thus, storage offers a way to flatten out the peaks and valleys of supply and prevent disruptive economics.

Today, utility-scale storage (in front of the meter) accounts for the majority of installed storage capacity, providing numerous system functions, and is also proving an effective way to complement peaker plants. Behind-the-meter storage allows customers to store the electricity generated by their rooftop solar panels and use it later when needed—for example, after the sun sets. Some estimates indicate that almost half of the annual deployments of energy storage by 2020 will be non-utility-scale storage.

Projections estimate that demand for energy storage, excluding pumped hydro, will increase from 400 MWh globally in 2015 to nearly 50 GWh in 2025. Lithium ion batteries will make up most of the market, and those are likely to become more economical as vast quantities are developed and deployed for use in electric vehicles, a market where the demand for these batteries could reach 293 GWh by 2025.

Storage is becoming cheaper as a result of advances in battery technologies and is achieving higher capacities that will allow for larger scale deployment. With current projections, utility-scale storage could be a viable alternative to peaker plants by 2023. As battery costs decline, the cost of storage could reach parity with grid power in the late 2020s—an inflection point after which grid operators will be able to offer the flexibility of peaker plants by tapping the stored output of renewables.

Challenges

Structural barriers include the lack of price signals to encourage distributed storage, no clear definition of storage as an asset and poor integration with current planning processes. Effective storage depends on storing and discharging electrons at optimal times, and that in turn depends on clear and automatic pricing signals sent to smart storage systems. Currently, most electric systems lack such real-time pricing signals at the customer level.

At the grid level, ownership structures and potential returns have not been consistently and clearly designed, and this uncertainty delays potential investments in grid assets. Storage can also provide a solution to some local congestion challenges at the distribution level and therefore defer or avoid potential upgrades in grid infrastructure. However, storage is typically not included in system planning processes and thus its impact cannot be fully realized.

Opportunities

Storage will help decarbonize generation by smoothing out the supply curve and paving the way for more renewable generation. The use of storage in commercial and industrial environments has boomed in recent years. However, storage achieves its greatest value at the system level when it is connected to the grid and a full set of services can be realized at various levels, such as network management services (frequency regulation, voltage support), utility services (resource adequacy, congestion relief) and customer services (backup power, demand charge reduction). Coupled with price signals, it can provide additional benefits in the form of rate arbitrage and deferred capital investment necessary to upgrade the grid. Some providers of distributed energy storage are combining big data, predictive analytics and advanced energy storage to reduce electricity costs for customers and simultaneously aggregate these assets to provide capacity to the grid when demand is peaking.

Energy Efficiency

Product innovation and energy efficiency programmes have combined to make most consumer and industrial power products dramatically more efficient than they were just a few years ago. In IEA countries, investments in efficiency since 1990 have helped to avoid electric consumption equivalent to about 5 million homes each year. Energy consumption for lighting has fallen more than 75% as compact fluorescents and LEDs replace incandescent lamps.

In the US, products with the EPA's Energy Star label certifying their efficiency make up 46% of new refrigerators, 84% of new dishwashers, 93% of new LCD monitors, 53% of new computers and 67% of new compact fluorescent lamps.

Challenges

Despite this apparent success, adoption of energy efficient products remains challenged by long replacement cycles for appliances and equipment (nine or more years) and largely based on technological innovation and incentives. It will take more than 25 years to replace the refrigerators in the US with more efficient ones, as nearly half of new refrigerators are energy efficient and replacement cycles take about 13 years.

Standards and mandates have proven effective in speeding up replacement cycles, but not all energy efficiency programmes have been equally successful. Some have seen limited adoption and impact, especially downstream programmes that rely on residential customer adoption. For example, Green Deal in the UK, which provided loans to fund energy efficiency improvements, saw less than 1% of loan up-take in the first 16 months and funding was later stopped. Top-down programs have been more effective, such as Energy Star and programs that encourage LED lighting.

Opportunities

Despite the limitations, energy efficiency products and programmes are worth pursuing because they are often the lowest cost way to meet resource needs. Avoiding a kilowatt-hour of demand is typically cheaper than supplying that demand by any other available resource. With an average price of about 2 to 3 cents per kWh including participant costs, energy efficiency is a cost-effective resource and is significantly less expensive than investing in additional generation. The IEA estimates that every dollar spent on energy efficiency avoids more than $2 in supply investments.

Demand Response

Demand response creates flexibility by providing price and volume signals and sometimes financial incentives to adjust the level of demand and generation resources (consumption, distributed generation and storage) at strategic times of the day.

As such, it is a critical resource for a cost-effective transition to a low-carbon electricity system. Energy policies around the world increasingly acknowledge the importance of demand response and are beginning to solve the challenges that hinder its full uptake. As more distributed energy resources (DERs) come online, demand-response programmes may become even more flexible and by some estimates could reduce necessary annual investments in US grid infrastructure by 10%. Many programmes have targeted commercial and industrial customers since the residential sector can be more difficult due to a range of factors, including high acquisition costs for individuals and the limited range of flexibility available to them. However, new smarter devices, such as pre-cooling air conditioners, smart refrigerators and shallow lighting that can respond to automated price signals, as well as the progress of digitalization that is enhancing the technical capabilities of aggregation, are helping make demand response programmes easier even for residential customers.

Public and private efforts demonstrating these newer technologies are proving successful. In Gotland, Sweden, several hundred electricity customers participated in a programme that integrated price signals (for example, lower prices at off-peak times) with a smartphone app that allowed them to choose between four pre-set levels. At the start of the programme, 23% of total electricity consumption occurred during the five most expensive hours; this dropped to 19% and 20% in the first and second year of the programme. Additionally, companies have begun to offer more advanced demand-response programmes. Opower's programme alerts customers about peak times through text or email messages. Enernoc offers a turnkey demand-response programme to utilities and grid operators, as well as commercial and industrial companies.

Challenges

Three main challenges have hindered the uptake of demand response: lack of market integration (including market access, definition of standardized processes for measurement, verification and settlement, unclear role or not allowed independent aggregation), absence of price signals and inconvenience.

Opportunities

Demand flexibility creates value for customers and the grid by shrinking customer bills (by as much as 40%), reducing peak demand and shifting consumption to lower price, off-peak hours. Demand flexibility also can help providers, in some cases, to avoid or defer investments in central generation, transmission and distribution, and peaker plants. The global demand response market is estimated to be 68.8 gigawatts by 2018—capacity will be able to be time shifted.

[...]

Conclusions

Grid edge technologies are paving the way towards a new energy system that will unlock significant economic and societal benefits. However, there is a great risk for value destruction if the system fails to efficiently capture the value of distributed energy resources, which could leave generation or network assets stranded and see customers defect from the grid. This risk represents one more reason to identify and take the right actions that will accelerate and make the transition cost effective.

The speed of adoption and the success in shaping the transformation in the most beneficial way for the society and the system overall will depend on a broad range of factors, which fall under four main dimensions: regulation, infrastructure, business models and customer engagement. The public and private sectors will need to contribute to successfully accelerate adoption of grid edge technologies, as neither can do it alone.

Policy-makers will have to redesign the regulatory paradigm, adapting the network revenue model and tariffs, planning the electricity system (taking into account both utility scale and distributed energy resources), and using price signals.

Regulators will have to foster agile governance by adopting stable long-term regulation that includes faster reaction cycles, involving more stakeholders and including an urban regulatory dimension.

The private sector will have to acknowledge the new reality of a digital, customer-empowered, transactive electricity system by embracing new business models and simplifying and redesigning the experience of residential, commercial and industrial customers.

All stakeholders will have to deploy enabling infrastructure that is flexible, open and interoperable. Public-private partnerships will help build enabling infrastructure, even if it is not yet commercially viable and thus requires initial public intervention.

Emerging markets that may be less encumbered by existing infrastructure, investments, or system structure may have the opportunity to leapfrog some of these challenges and head straight to mass adoption of these new technologies.

The World Economic Forum examined the opportunities and challenges inherent in the advent of grid edge technologies and believes these are exciting technologies that offer more choice for customers, greater efficiency and better economics for stakeholders in the electricity ecosystem. The findings and recommendations in this report will be useful for policy-makers, regulators and private enterprise as they work to accelerate the adoption of these technologies and the positive changes they offer to electricity markets worldwide.

Biomass and Its Environmental Impacts

US Energy Information Administration

The US Energy Information Administration collects, analyzes, and disseminates independent and impartial energy information to promote sound policymaking, efficient markets, and public understanding of energy and its interaction with the economy and the environment.

Biomass and biofuels made from biomass are alternative energy sources to fossil fuels—coal, petroleum, and natural gas. Burning either fossil fuels or biomass releases carbon dioxide (CO_2), a greenhouse gas. However, the plants that are the source of biomass capture a nearly equivalent amount of CO_2 through photosynthesis while they are growing, which can make biomass a carbon-neutral energy source.

Burning Wood

Using wood, wood pellets, and charcoal for heating and cooking can replace fossil fuels and may result in lower CO_2 emissions overall. Wood can be harvested from forests, woodlots that have to be thinned, or from urban trees that fall down or have to be cut down.

Wood smoke contains harmful pollutants like carbon monoxide and particulate matter. Modern wood-burning stoves, pellet stoves, and fireplace inserts can reduce the amount of particulates from burning wood. Wood and charcoal are major cooking and heating fuels in poor countries, but if people harvest the wood faster than trees can grow, it causes deforestation. Planting fast-growing trees for fuel and using fuel-efficient cooking stoves can help slow deforestation and improve the environment.

"Biomass and the Environment," US Energy Information Administration, February 2, 2017.

Burning Municipal Solid Waste (MSW) or Wood Waste

Burning municipal solid waste (MSW, or garbage) to produce energy in waste-to-energy plants means that less waste is buried in landfills. On the other hand, burning garbage produces air pollution and releases the chemicals and substances in the waste into the air. Some of these chemicals can be hazardous to people and the environment if they are not properly controlled.

The US Environmental Protection Agency (EPA) applies strict environmental rules to waste-to-energy plants, and requires that waste-to-energy plants use air pollution control devices such as scrubbers, fabric filters, and electrostatic precipitators to capture air pollutants.

Scrubbers clean emissions from waste-to-energy facilities by spraying a liquid into the combustion gases to neutralize the acids present in the stream of emissions. Fabric filters and electrostatic precipitators also remove particles from the combustion gases. The particles—called fly ash—are then mixed with the ash that is removed from the bottom of the waste-to-energy furnace.

A waste-to-energy furnace burns at high temperatures (1,800°F to 2,000°F), which breaks down the chemicals in MSW into simpler, less harmful compounds.

Disposing Ash from Waste-to-Energy Plants

Ash can contain high concentrations of various metals that were present in the original waste. Textile dyes, printing inks, and ceramics, for example, may contain lead and cadmium.

Separating waste before burning can solve part of the problem. Because batteries are the largest source of lead and cadmium in municipal waste, they should not be included in regular trash. Florescent light bulbs should also not be put in regular trash because they contain small amounts of mercury.

The EPA tests ash from waste-to-energy plants to make sure that it is not hazardous. The test looks for chemicals and metals that could contaminate ground water. Some MSW landfills use ash that is considered safe as a cover layer for their landfills, and some MSW ash is used to make concrete blocks and bricks.

Collecting Landfill Gas or Biogas

Biogas forms as a result of biological processes in sewage treatment plants, waste landfills, and livestock manure management systems. Biogas is composed mainly of methane (a greenhouse gas) and CO_2. Many facilities that produce biogas capture it and burn the methane for heat or to generate electricity. This electricity is considered renewable, and in many states, contributes to meeting state renewable portfolio standards (RPS). This electricity may replace electricity generation from fossil fuels and can result in a net reduction in CO_2 emissions. Burning methane produces CO_2, but because methane is a stronger greenhouse gas than CO_2, the overall greenhouse effect is lower.

Liquid Biofuels: Ethanol and Biodiesel

Biofuels are transportation fuels such as ethanol and biodiesel. The federal government promotes ethanol use as a transportation fuel to help reduce oil imports and CO_2 emissions. In 2007, the government set a target to use 36 billion gallons of biofuels by 2022. As a result, nearly all gasoline now sold in the United States contains some ethanol.

Biofuels may be carbon-neutral because the plants that are used to make biofuels (such as corn and sugarcane for ethanol and soy beans and palm oil trees for biodiesel) absorb CO_2 as they grow and may offset the CO_2 emissions when biofuels are produced and burned.

Growing plants for biofuels is controversial because the land, fertilizers, and energy for growing biofuel crops could be used to grow food crops instead. In some parts of the world, large areas of natural vegetation and forests have been cut down to grow sugar cane for ethanol and soybeans and palm oil trees for biodiesel. The US government supports efforts to develop alternative sources of biomass that do not compete with food crops and that use less fertilizer and pesticides than corn and sugar cane. The US government also supports methods to produce ethanol that require less energy than conventional fermentation. Ethanol can also be made from waste paper, and biodiesel can be made from waste grease and oils and even algae.

Ethanol and gasoline-ethanol blends burn cleaner and have higher octane ratings than pure gasoline, but they have higher *evaporative emissions* from fuel tanks and dispensing equipment. These evaporative emissions contribute to the formation of harmful, ground-level ozone and smog. Gasoline requires extra processing to reduce evaporative emissions before it is blended with ethanol. Biodiesel combustion produces fewer sulfur oxides, less particulate matter, less carbon monoxide, and fewer unburned and other hydrocarbons, but it does produce more nitrogen oxide than petroleum diesel.

The Many Variables of Renewable Energy

Jeremy Williams

Jeremy Williams is a freelance writer with a focus on sustainability, climate change, and post-growth economics. He writes for the blog Make Wealth History, *which emphasizes providing an equal playing field for countries at all levels of development, whether developed or developing.*

Something quietly remarkable happened in Germany recently. As the country enjoyed a sunny May day, its extensive solar power installations recorded their best ever performance. Solar power hit a new international record of 22GW, equivalent to 20 nuclear power stations. At one point on Saturday, Germany was almost 50% solar powered.

There's lots I could say about Germany's power strategy, both positive and negative, but what I wanted to highlight was the way that renewable energy was accommodated in the system. Averaged over a year, solar power only accounts for 3.5% or so of Germany's electricity generation, yet at the end of May there were days when solar power was providing ten times that. So far, the national grid has proved it is perfectly capable of handling these extremes.

This illustrated one of the big challenges to renewable energy: they are intermittent energy sources. A coal power station can run as long as you have coal to shovel into its furnaces. Wind power only operates when the wind blows, and solar photovoltaics need cloudless skies to reach their full capacity. Surely, say the critics, too much renewable energy puts us at the mercy of the elements? The greater the percentage of wind or solar in our energy mix, the more likely we are to end up with rolling blackouts. It's a logical question, but there are solutions.

"How to Deal With Intermittent Energy Sources," by Jeremy Williams, Make Wealth History, June 8, 2012. Reprinted by permission.

The Grid

The first and biggest answer to this problem is the grid. Power stations feed into a national grid that balances inputs and outputs across the whole country. When demand rises, new capacity is brought online. At night, demand drops off and supply drops accordingly. It's a highly versatile system, able to handle massive spikes in demand. The famous example is half-time during big football matches. The whistle blows, and everyone goes into the kitchen to switch on their kettles for a cup of tea, or opens their fridge for another beer. The National Grid refers to these as "tv-pickups" and plans ahead for them so that the lights don't go out.

It's easy to take functioning power infrastructure for granted. If you've lived off-grid or in a developing country, you'll know the luxury of not having to think about it. When I lived in Madagascar, the power levels dropped so low at night that we couldn't switch on the TV. If you wanted to watch something that night, you had to remember to turn it on at about five o'clock and leave it on standby. By the time it had got dark and everyone had turned on their lights, there would be enough power to run it but not to turn it on. By day, you had to holler if you were going to boil the kettle. If you forgot, there would be wails from the office as someone lost their homework as the computer blinked off.

Those sorts of eccentricities don't happen in Britain. At least not any more. The idea of balancing power supplies across the country goes back to 1926, and today the grid incorporates 181 major power stations and thousands of smaller installations. This infrastructure allows us to plug in a variety of variable energy sources, and the broader the network, the easier it becomes.

The Supergrid

You can broaden the network beyond our own borders too. Interconnectors already link our grid with France, Ireland and the Netherlands. There are plans to build links to Norway and Belgium too, and a feasibility study was launched last month to see if we could connect to Denmark. Iceland has far more geothermal capacity than it can use itself, and is investigating ways to export it to Britain.

None of this infrastructure is cheap, but the fact that we already have three international links proves that it isn't prohibitively expensive either. Whether we can afford a Europe-wide grid with links to North Africa is another matter, but you can see the advantages of spreading the net as wide as possible. If the sun isn't shining here right now, it might be in Devon. It might be a calm day in London, but the wind is blowing in Scotland. Expand that principle south to Spain and north to Sweden, and you've got a wide variety of conditions.

Stabilising Demand

I've already mentioned the issue of peaks in demand. Some of these are unusual, like football matches. Others are regular, when people get up and make breakfast, or get home from work in the evening and turn on their lights and cook their supper. Coal power is one of the easiest ways to deal with these large peaks, as they can be switched on quickly. There are renewable energy equivalents, using biomass and incineration, but a better approach would be to avoid the extremes in the first place.

That be done through more efficient technologies—if everyone is switching on low-energy light bulbs at twilight, that's a much lower step in demand than everyone switching on an incandescent. Another way of stabilising demand is through smart appliances that can read demand and respond accordingly. Fridges don't run constantly, but maintain a steady temperature by switching the cooling mechanism on when needed. A smart fridge would time its cooling cycles to periods of low demand. A smart washing machine would automatically run off-peak when energy prices are cheapest. Samsung, LG and others already offer appliances with this kind of technology.

Energy Storage

Those living off-grid with their own solar or wind power rely on batteries to make sure that they capture energy when its there, and can use it later. That would be pretty useful in the national grid too, if we could store the solar energy from a sunny day to use it at night. Currently there's no form of battery big enough to do that, but there are a few other options. One is pumped storage hydropower. When energy is cheap, water is pumped uphill to fill a reservoir. When needed, gates can be opened and it runs back downhill through turbines, generating electricity. This is the renewable energy way of dealing with demand spikes, and also a way of storing intermittent sources. Dinorwig power station is housed underground inside a Welsh mountain, and can bring 1.8GW of power online in 12 seconds.

If you haven't got a suitable lake, the same thing could be achieved with rail cars, according to a California company. They're developing a model where surplus energy is used to haul heavy rail cars uphill when wind or solar power is running at full capacity. When it drops off, the cars are released to roll back downhill, generating electricity on the way.

You can also "bank" energy in the ocean, taking advantage of the pressure of the deep sea. A team at MIT suggest that large hollow concrete spheres could be sunk on the seabed near offshore wind turbines. Excess energy would be used to pump out the spheres. When the wind dropped, water would rush back in through a turbine.

Another form of energy storage is solar thermal. I've written about it before so I won't go into detail here, but it essentially stores heat in molten salt, and allows solar power stations to carry on generating electricity through the night. This turns solar energy into a form of constant renewable energy.

Constant Renewable Energy

Speaking of which, wind and sunshine are intermittent, but there are other natural forces that are much more predictable.

Hydropower is one such source, using the steady flow of rivers. There are countries in the world that generate all their electricity from hydropower, and are thus enjoying 100% renewable energy. Hydropower is often overlooked because while it is renewable and clean, it isn't always environmentally benign and has large capital costs. Large dams are often hugely destructive and displace entire communities. But there is good hydropower too, and I may have to dedicate a separate post to it.

There's also a whole lot of energy to be sourced from the sea. Harnessing wave power is one approach, but doesn't count as a constant renewable source because waves are variable. Tidal power does count however, as there's always a tide. So far, tidal power requires a barrage across a suitable estuary. Like dams on land, dams across estuaries are just as controversial—see the running debate about the Severn Barrage. But there are simpler and smaller ways to harness tidal power too, placing turbines on the sea bed, or using the vertical movement of the tides rather than the vertical. Ecotricity are trialling a hybrid sea technology that uses sea swells to pump water onshore, which is a lot simpler than generating the electricity out on the open sea.

Geothermal provides another source of constant renewable energy. Britain has limited geothermal capacity, and is more useful for providing heat than electricity, but there is still untapped potential. The main reason that geothermal hasn't been pursued in Britain is that it hasn't been economical so far, but as the price of energy rises, it is becoming more viable. The Eden Project is pioneering a geothermal plant in Cornwall, the first of what it hopes will be a fairly substantial contribution from Cornwall's "hot rocks."

Biomass and anaerobic digestion (biogas) are two more renewable energy sources that are often overlooked. Biomass is best reserved for smaller and more localised energy generation, and the current practice of co-firing biomass with coal is a short term option. Biogas is generated from waste, so it doubles up as a useful way of dealing with rubbish otherwise destined for landfill, and its main waste product is a liquid that can be used as fertiliser.

Lowering Energy Use

Even with these various technologies and techniques, renewable energy can never be a direct swap for fossil fuels. Coal, oil and gas are very dense forms of energy, and deliver a high energy return for energy invested. Renewable energy cannot match it, and if we are to rely on renewable energy more in the future, we will have to reduce our energy use. That's entirely possible, given how inefficient our houses are, how much electricity is lost in transmission and how low our standards are for appliances.

Quite how far we need to reduce our energy use is debateable, but those assuming we can expand it or carry on as usual aren't paying attention. The Zero Carbon Britain report, which aims for 100% renewable energy by 2030, assumes a 55% reduction.

In summary, there are ways of managing the intermittent output of certain renewable energy sources. It is a challenge, but it is not an insurmountable obstacle.

The Environmental Impacts of Wind Power

Union of Concerned Scientists

The Union of Concerned Scientists develops and implements innovative and practical solutions to the planet's most pressing problems, including global warming, finding sustainable methods of food development and transport, and reducing the threat of nuclear war.

Harnessing power from the wind is one of the cleanest and most sustainable ways to generate electricity as it produces no toxic pollution or global warming emissions. Wind is also abundant, inexhaustible, and affordable, which makes it a viable and large-scale alternative to fossil fuels.

Despite its vast potential, there are a variety of environmental impacts associated with wind power generation that should be recognized and mitigated.

Land Use

The land use impact of wind power facilities varies substantially depending on the site: wind turbines placed in flat areas typically use more land than those located in hilly areas. However, wind turbines do not occupy all of this land; they must be spaced approximately 5 to 10 rotor diameters apart (a rotor diameter is the diameter of the wind turbine blades). Thus, the turbines themselves and the surrounding infrastructure (including roads and transmission lines) occupy a small portion of the total area of a wind facility.

A survey by the National Renewable Energy Laboratory of large wind facilities in the United States found that they use between 30 and 141 acres per megawatt of power output capacity (a typical new utility-scale wind turbine is about 2 megawatts). However,

"Environmental Impacts of Wind Power," Union of Concerned Scientists (WWW. UCSUSA.ORG), March 5, 2013. Reprinted by permission.

less than 1 acre per megawatt is disturbed permanently and less than 3.5 acres per megawatt are disturbed temporarily during construction.[1] The remainder of the land can be used for a variety of other productive purposes, including livestock grazing, agriculture, highways, and hiking trails.[2] Alternatively, wind facilities can be sited on brownfields (abandoned or underused industrial land) or other commercial and industrial locations, which significantly reduces concerns about land use.[3]

Offshore wind facilities, which are currently not in operation in the United States but may become more common, require larger amounts of space because the turbines and blades are bigger than their land-based counterparts. Depending on their location, such offshore installations may compete with a variety of other ocean activities, such as fishing, recreational activities, sand and gravel extraction, oil and gas extraction, navigation, and aquaculture. Employing best practices in planning and siting can help minimize potential land use impacts of offshore and land-based wind projects.[4]

Wildlife and Habitat

The impact of wind turbines on wildlife, most notably on birds and bats, has been widely document and studied. A recent National Wind Coordinating Committee (NWCC) review of peer-reviewed research found evidence of bird and bat deaths from collisions with wind turbines and due to changes in air pressure caused by the spinning turbines, as well as from habitat disruption. The NWCC concluded that these impacts are relatively low and do not pose a threat to species populations.[5]

Additionally, research into wildlife behavior and advances in wind turbine technology have helped to reduce bird and bat deaths. For example, wildlife biologists have found that bats are most active when wind speeds are low. Using this information, the Bats and Wind Energy Cooperative concluded that keeping wind turbines motionless during times of low wind speeds could reduce bat deaths by more than half without significantly affecting power production.[6] Other wildlife impacts can be mitigated through better siting of wind turbines. The US Fish and Wildlife Services has played a leadership role in this effort by convening an advisory group including representatives from industry, state and tribal governments, and nonprofit organizations that made comprehensive recommendations on appropriate wind farm siting and best management practices.[7]

Offshore wind turbines can have similar impacts on marine birds, but as with onshore wind turbines, the bird deaths associated with offshore wind are minimal. Wind farms located offshore will also impact fish and other marine wildlife. Some studies suggest that turbines may actually increase fish populations by acting as artificial reefs. The impact will vary from site to site, and therefore proper research and monitoring systems are needed for each offshore wind facility.[8]

Public Health and Community

Sound and visual impact are the two main public health and community concerns associated with operating wind turbines. Most of the sound generated by wind turbines is aerodynamic, caused by the movement of turbine blades through the air. There is also mechanical sound generated by the turbine itself. Overall sound levels depend on turbine design and wind speed.

Some people living close to wind facilities have complained about sound and vibration issues, but industry and government-sponsored studies in Canada and Australia have found that these issues do not adversely impact public health.[9] However, it is important for wind turbine developers to take these community concerns seriously by following "good neighbor" best practices for siting turbines and initiating open dialogue with affected community members. Additionally, technological advances, such as minimizing blade surface imperfections and using sound-absorbent materials can reduce wind turbine noise.[10]

Under certain lighting conditions, wind turbines can create an effect known as shadow flicker. This annoyance can be minimized with careful siting, planting trees or installing window awnings, or curtailing wind turbine operations when certain lighting conditions exist.[11]

The Federal Aviation Administration (FAA) requires that large wind turbines, like all structures over 200 feet high, have white or red lights for aviation safety. However, the FAA recently determined that as long as there are no gaps in lighting greater than a half-mile, it is not necessary to light each tower in a multi-turbine wind project. Daytime lighting is unnecessary as long as the turbines are painted white.

When it comes to aesthetics, wind turbines can elicit strong reactions. To some people, they are graceful sculptures; to others, they are eyesores that compromise the natural landscape. Whether a community is willing to accept an altered skyline in return for cleaner power should be decided in an open public dialogue.[12]

Water Use

There is no water impact associated with the operation of wind turbines. As in all manufacturing processes, some water is used to manufacture steel and cement for wind turbines.

Life-Cycle Global Warming Emissions

While there are no global warming emissions associated with operating wind turbines, there are emissions associated with other stages of a wind turbine's life-cycle, including materials production, materials transportation, on-site construction and assembly, operation and maintenance, and decommissioning and dismantlement.

Estimates of total global warming emissions depend on a number of factors, including wind speed, percent of time the wind is blowing, and the material composition of the wind turbine.[13] Most estimates of wind turbine life-cycle global warming emissions are between 0.02 and 0.04 pounds of carbon dioxide equivalent per kilowatt-hour. To put this into context, estimates of life-cycle global warming emissions for natural gas generated electricity are between

0.6 and 2 pounds of carbon dioxide equivalent per kilowatt-hour and estimates for coal-generated electricity are 1.4 and 3.6 pounds of carbon dioxide equivalent per kilowatt-hour.[14]

References

[1] Denholm, P., M. Hand, M. Jackson, and S. Ong. 2009. Land-use requirements of modern wind power plants in the United States. Golden, CO: National Renewable Energy Laboratory.

[2] National Renewable Energy Laboratory (NREL). 2012. Renewable Electricity Futures Study. Hand, M.M.; Baldwin, S.; DeMeo, E.; Reilly, J.M.; Mai, T.; Arent, D.; Porro, G.; Meshek, M.; Sandor, D. eds. 4 vols. NREL/TP-6A20-52409. Golden, CO: National Renewable Energy Laboratory.

[3] National Renewable Energy Laboratory (NREL). June 14, 2010. Brownfields' Bright Spot: Solar and Wind Energy. Online at http://www.nrel.gov/news/features/feature_detail.cfm/feature_id=1530

[4] Michel, J.; Dunagan, H.; Boring, C.; Healy, E.; Evans, W.; Dean, J.; McGillis, A.; Hain, J. 2007. Worldwide Synthesis and Analysis of Existing Information Regarding Environmental Effects of Alternative Energy Uses on the Outer Continental Shelf. MMS 2007-038. Prepared by Research Planning and ICF International. Herndon, VA: US Department of the Interior, Minerals Management Service.

[5] National Wind Coordinating Committee (NWCC). 2010. Wind turbine interactions with birds, bats, and their habitats: A summary of research results and priority questions.

[6] Arnett, E.B., M.M.P. Huso, J.P. Hayes, and M. Schirmacher. 2010. Effectiveness of changing wind turbine cut-in speed to reduce bat fatalities at wind facilities. A final report submitted to the Bats and Wind Energy Cooperative. Austin, TX: Bat Conservation International.

[7] Fish and Wildlife Service (FSW). 2010. Recommendations of the wind turbine guidelines advisory committee.

[8] Michel, et al. 2007.

[9] Chief Medical Officer of Heath of Ontario. 2010. The potential health impact of wind turbines. Toronto, Ontario: Ontario Ministry of Health and Long Term Care.

American Wind Energy Association (AWEA) and the Canadian Wind Energy Association (CanWEA). 2009. Wind turbine sound and health effects: An expert panel review.

National Health and Medical Research Council (NHMRC). 2010. Wind turbines and health: A rapid review of the evidence. Canberra, Australia: National Health and Medical Research Council.

[10] Bastasch, M.; van Dam, J.; Søndergaard, B.; Rogers, A. 2006. Wind Turbine Noise – An Overview. Canadian Acoustics (34:2), 7–15.

[11] National Renewable Energy Laboratory (NREL). 2012. Renewable Electricity Futures Study.

[12] Union of Concerned Scientists. Tapping into Wind.

[13] National Academy of Sciences. 2010. Electricity from Renewable Resources: Status, Prospects, and Impediments.

[14] IPCC, 2011: IPCC Special Report on Renewable Energy Sources and Climate Change Mitigation. Prepared by Working Group III of the Intergovernmental Panel on Climate Change [O. Edenhofer, R. Pichs-Madruga, Y. Sokona, K. Seyboth, P. Matschoss, S. Kadner, T. Zwickel, P. Eickemeier, G. Hansen, S. Schlömer, C. von Stechow (eds)]. Cambridge University Press, Cambridge, United Kingdom and New York, NY, USA, 1075 pp. (Chapter 7 & 9).

Is It Possible for Renewables to Be Widely Used Around the World?

International Surge in Hydropower Development

World Energy Council

The World Energy Council is an impartial network of organizations dedicated to the promotion of affordable, stable, and environmentally sensitive energy systems for the benefit of all peoples.

There has been a major upsurge in hydropower development globally in recent years. The total installed capacity has grown by 39% from 2005 to 2015, with an average growth rate of nearly 4% per year. The rise has been concentrated in emerging markets where hydropower offers not only clean energy, but also provides water services, energy security and facilitates regional cooperation and economic development. The drivers for the upsurge in hydropower development include the increased demand for electricity, energy storage, flexibility of generation, freshwater management, and climate change mitigation and adaptation solutions. On the one hand, there has been significant progress in terms of sustainability practices in the sector and acceptance by external stakeholders such as NGOs and the financial community, which had previously opposed the development of some new projects. On the other hand, criticism of hydropower continues in some stakeholder groups, whose views are mainly biased by past negative experiences and a lack of acknowledgement of sustainable projects successfully built more recently.

As a mature technology, hydropower provides over 16% of global electricity production. Since 2004, hydropower development has been on the increase, as emerging markets recognise the benefits that it can bring. In addition to low-cost electricity supply, hydropower provides energy storage and other ancillary services that contribute to the more efficient management of the electricity supply system and balancing of the grid.

"World Energy Resources Hydropower," World Energy Council, 2016. Reprinted by permission.

An important new driver for global development is hydropower's role as a flexible generation asset as well as an energy storage technology. Storage hydropower (including pumped storage) represents 99% of the world's operational electricity storage. With the increased deployment of variable renewable energy technologies such as wind and solar, hydropower is increasingly recognised as an important system management asset capable of ensuring reliable renewable supply.

Infrastructure for hydropower projects is also used for freshwater management, and projects with reservoir storage generally provide a variety of value-added services. For example, in addition to providing reliable energy supply, hydropower typically brings a variety of macroeconomic benefits such as water supply, flood protection, drought management, navigation, irrigation and recreation. As water management infrastructure, it is also expected to play an increasing role in climate change adaptation. It will be called upon to help respond to expected increases in extreme weather events, including more intense and frequent flood incidents and longer periods of drought.

These multiple services and benefits have reinvigorated interest in hydropower and have altered perceptions of its importance. There have also been significant advances in sustainable development practices in the sector—the sector now has a widely recognised and broadly supported tool to assess hydropower project sustainability, as well as to promote improved sustainability performance across the sector. These factors have combined to improve acceptance and willingness of policymakers and the financial sector to engage in hydropower development, through enabling policy frameworks and, crucially, providing investment and financial support to both public and private entities.

Global Status

Hydropower is the leading renewable source for electricity generation globally, supplying 71% of all renewable electricity. Reaching 1,064 GW of installed capacity in 2016, it generated 16.4% of the world's electricity from all sources.

Since 2004, there has been a resurgence in hydropower development, particularly in emerging markets and less developed countries. Significant new development is concentrated in the markets of Asia (particularly China), Latin America and Africa. In these regions, hydropower offers an opportunity to supply electricity to under-served populations and a growing industrial base, while at the same time providing a range of complementary benefits associated with multi-purpose projects.

From 1999 through 2005, hydropower development was largely halted worldwide, reflecting the impact of the World Commission on Dams (WCD), which was convened to review the development effectiveness of large dams and develop guidelines for the development of new dams. The report, published by the WCD in 2000, challenged existing practices and proposed stringent guidelines for dams, which in turn caused a sharp decrease in investments while the sector and the financial community considered how to respond to new standards and expectations.

From 2005 onwards, hydropower development has seen an upswing in development, which can be attributed in part to the impact of intensive efforts by the International Hydropower Association (IHA) and a multi-stakeholder range of partners in promoting greater sustainability through the development and use of the Hydropower Sustainability Assessment Protocol. The protocol provides an international common language on how these considerations can be addressed at all phases of a project's lifestyle: planning, preparation, implementation and operation. Protocol assessments are delivered by fully accredited assessors who have previous experience of the hydropower sector or relevant sustainability issues. To receive accreditation, assessors must participate in at least two assessments as trainees prior to attending an accreditation course.

Additionally, growing investments in and by emerging economies (i.e. BRICS, particularly China), continued interest in renewable energy, particularly with storage capacity. Participation in Carbon Markets / Renewable Energy Credits has also contributed to the upswing.

In recent years China has taken centre stage for hydropower capacity, accounting for 26% of global installed capacity in 2015, far ahead of USA (8.4%), Brazil (7.6%) and Canada (6.5%). China has strengthened its dominant position by adding 19 GW in 2015, almost three times the new capacity of the next five countries combined.

Capacity additions in 2015 have strengthened China's lead, with new developments progressing at Baihetan (16 GW) and Wudongde (10.2 GW). Total capacity in China is expected to reach 350 GW of pure hydropower and 70 GW of pumped storage by 2020.

Beyond China, significant new deployment took place in the emerging markets of Asia including concentrations in Russia, India, Turkey and Vietnam. Asia has the largest unutilised potential, estimated at 7,195 TWh/year, making it the likely leading market for future development. Rapid, concentrated development is expected to continue in India, Turkey, Bhutan and Nepal.

Latin America is another key market for hydropower development. Brazil leads the continent in both installed capacity and new capacity additions, with 91.8 GW installed capacity in total. Hydropower forms the backbone of Brazil's electricity system, supplying 62% in 2015 of the country's needs, although this figure is expected to decline due to a reducing number of sites available to develop and increased investment in fossil fuel generation. However, Brazil looks set to continue hydropower development with plans for construction of up to 19 GW in the next ten years. Other Latin American countries with significant hydropower capacity include Argentina, Chile, Colombia, Paraguay, Peru, Venezuela and Ecuador.

Africa is expected to be a major market for future hydropower activity. With the average electrification rates at only 45% in 2012, hydropower offers real opportunities for providing electricity on the continent using largely local or regional resources. Significant undeveloped potential remains across all of Africa, with only an estimated 9% of reported hydropower potential developed to date. In particular, the markets of the Democratic Republic of the Congo, Angola, Ethiopia and Cameroon have significant undeveloped potential. Regional African co-operation bodies, including the Eastern Africa Power Pool, the West African Power Pool and the Southern African Power Pool, have the potential to drive further development of hydropower where domestic resources can be developed for export to neighbouring countries with strong demand.

Global Potential

There are many opportunities for hydropower development throughout the world and although there is no clear consensus, estimates indicate the availability of approximately 10,000 TWh/year of unutilised hydropower potential worldwide. How much of that will be developed is a matter of market conditions, government policy and the emergence of other competing renewable options, such as solar PV, wind and biomass. Power pools, increased bilateral trade in electricity, and new customers demanding green energy can enable further growth in hydropower.

Various scenarios look at potential future development, with some indicating a potential to reach up to 2000–2050 GW of installed hydropower capacity by 2050.

[…]

Economics and Markets

With the increasing multi-purpose use of freshwater reservoirs and the growing role of the private sector, it is important to analyse both economic and financial performance of hydropower developments.

Investment in hydropower has traditionally been within the realm of the public sector, as hydropower projects are major infrastructure investments. More recently, private players have entered the sector including public–private partnerships, in which risks are allocated to the party best able to manage it.

With regard to financial performance, like many other capital-intensive large infrastructure projects, hydropower has been subject to some criticism on the basis of cost and schedule overruns. However, there are many examples of projects that have been managed successfully from a cost and schedule perspective. For example, Hydro-Québec announced in December 2015 the commissioning of the second and final turbine of the 270 MW Romaine-1 station, eight months ahead of schedule.

Numerous studies have analysed the levelised cost of electricity (LCOE) of hydropower in comparison to other energy technologies. A study of 2,155 hydropower projects in the United States found that the LCOE ranged from a low of $0.012/kWh for additional capacity at an existing hydropower project, to a high of $0.19/kWh for a 1 MW small hydro project with a capacity factor of 30%. The weighted average cost of all the sites evaluated was $0.048/kWh. The LCOE of 80% of the projects was between $0.018 and $0.085/kWh.

The share of the electro-mechanical equipment costs in the total LCOE ranged from a low of 17% to a high of 50%, with typical values ranging from 21% to 31%. Civil works costs ranged from zero (for an existing project) to a high of 63%.

There are several approaches used in the power sector for the estimation of LCOE (IEA, IRENA, PwC). However, each project can have unique circumstances that can result in very specific costs that may fall outside of the typical range; e.g. if a partnership with local communities becomes a major element of capital cost.

Hydropower projects of all magnitudes have the similar financial profile of high capital cost, low operation and maintenance cost, no fuel cost and a relatively stable and sustained revenue stream. However, the scale of the project still plays a major role in the LCOE. Small-scale hydropower (installed capacity of less than 10 MW) may cost between US$0.2- 0.4/kWh, while a larger scheme of 300 MW and greater is likely to cost significantly less at approximately US$0.1/kWh, which considerably enhances the return to the investor.

It is important to note that the revenue stream from a hydropower project is more stable when a long-term power purchase agreements (PPA), bilateral contract or feed-in tariffs have been implemented prior to commissioning the facility. There is greater price risk in liberalised power markets, when not combined with any of the above. In the absence of long term contracts, hydropower operators will make generation decisions on the basis of shorter-term electricity prices, which can in many cases, bring higher returns relative to long-term PPAs, however, spot markets can also bring an element of risk to the hydropower operator which must be considered.

Historically, the decision for investment in hydropower is often made on an economic basis; however, another factor that has become increasingly important in the investment decision is the reputational risk of the project. The non-power services that hydropower can bring to a region often cannot be clearly quantified on a return on investment basis. For example, many hydropower projects offer an element of flood protection for the local region and the economic value lies in the value preservation and avoidance of damages. Although it is a highly valued benefit, there is no specific contribution to return on investment for this service. Other multi-purpose benefits include drought management, drinking water supply, irrigation, navigation and tourism, all of which typically do not offer clear and direct revenue streams to reservoir developers. Hydro projects also bring significant macroeconomic and societal benefits, such as employment opportunities, both during and after construction.

Economic and Financial Risks

As with any business, the key elements in the overall risk profile of an investment in large infrastructure projects are the profitability of the project, and the certainty of realising the expected returns. In the case of hydropower, reservoirs can extend to hundreds or even thousands of square kilometres, requiring detailed studies of the hydrology, geology, topography, environmental and social impacts. These studies, along with detailed proposals for the civil works and other technical aspects, form a significant portion of the early capital expenditures. This increases capital requirements, and therefore risk, as some of the studies are undertaken before there is any certainty around project authorisation.

During the construction phase, there is a reasonable certainty about the energy production and resulting revenue generation. At this stage, risk is generally due to cost containment from unforeseen problems.

During the operational phase, hydropower's low maintenance costs and no fuel requirement mean that most capital costs have already been incurred and revenues are typically stable. This, combined with the very long operating life of modern day hydropower facilities (more than 100 years), makes it an attractive prospect for jurisdictions capable of taking on the (long-term) financial risk of hydropower development. However, while risks decline significantly once the plant is put into service, operational risks can include changes in long-term hydrological conditions and more stringent regulatory environments.

Correlating with the changing risk profile through the planning, construction and operation stages of a project, the risk premium on financing for these projects also declines through each stage. In dynamic markets, risk and consequently reward, is taken on by different players throughout these distinct phases. With greater involvement of the private sector, there tend to be more changes in project ownership over the course of the project's lifecycle. Thus the cost of finance correlates with the risk of the specific lifecycle stage.

One of the latest developments in the hydropower sector aiming to assist the investors in the identification of risks and how these correlated throughout the lifetime of the project from planning to operation is the Hydropower Sustainability Assessment Protocol. This tool has been developed through the efforts of the International Hydropower Association in cooperation with a multi-stakeholder range of partners seeking to have the means to assess soundly the sustainability of a hydropower project, both holistically across particular sustainability topics.

Future Outlook

Private investment in the sector has increased over the past decades of high development, where markets have enabled such investment. Investment is also increasingly coming from new international players, both public and private. Chinese entities are investing heavily in Africa, East Asia, and South America. Norway's Statkraft and SN Power have investments in Turkey, Zambia, and Panama. Other notable investments have included South Korean investment in Nepal, Pakistan and the Philippines; Thailand's investment in Myanmar; and Iran's investment in Tajikistan.

Socio-Economics

Government Policies – Regulations and Incentives

Water, energy and climate policies have the potential to significantly influence decisions on hydropower developments.

For example, as a renewable energy, in some markets hydropower is eligible for price premiums such as feed-in-tariffs and for quota systems such as renewables obligations. Such government-funded incentive programmes have been shown to be positive drivers of deployment, as well as indirectly inducing hydropower development to help manage the variable output of large quantities of wind and solar coming online as a result of the same programmes. This is the case in Spain and Portugal, where a feed-in-tariff has spurred significant investment in wind and solar technologies, which in turn have led to increased development of pumped-storage hydropower to help balance the system.

It is important to note that hydropower development is highly subject to regulatory environments, related not just to energy, but also to water and environment. These policy spheres are often managed quite separately across various governments, leading to disjointed decision-making and conflicting signals. For example, in

Europe, the EU's 20-20- 20 legislation directs European countries to achieve a 20% share of renewables in the total final energy consumption by 2020. At the same time, the EU Water Framework Directive mandates actions that have in some cases been shown to deter consideration of hydropower. While targeted policies can be a factor in promoting hydropower, complementarity of policies across the suite of issues relevant to hydropower will also influence how it can be developed.

While there are several socio-economic drivers in play favouring hydropower development, there exist a number of policies hindering hydropower development. For example, despite the clear need for increased storage and other balancing services, most market systems do not appropriately reward these services. In Germany, existing pumped-storage projects have to pay transmission fees as final consumers during pumping operations (but not for generation). Policymakers are partly addressing this for new pumped-storage projects, which are exempted for 20 years. Additionally, any pumped-storage project, which was or is extended after 4 August 2011, by at least 7.5% of installed capacity or 5% of generation, is exempt for 10 years.

Another example of legislation hindering hydropower development is the prohibition of cross-ownership of generation and transmission assets, like in the case of several countries in Europe. The non-cross-ownership legislation is expected to lead to a more efficient use of regional and local electricity networks systems, and more effective performance of the market. Pump-storage hydropower plants are known to be a great asset for assisting to maintain a high quality level of the electricity system/network, and this type of hydropower can be further developed for this purpose. However, the markets do not yet reward fully the value of these benefits, thus posing a higher risk on the return-of-investment for the owner of this type of generation assets under the non-cross-ownership legislation. In contrast, in countries like China, where the legislation allows the state grid to own both transmission and generation assets, recognising the value of pumped-storage projects for a better operation of the electricity network, China is developing 41 GW of pump-storage projects. Alternatively, another possible solution for markets under the no-cross-ownership legislation, the development of pump-storage power plants could find a niche if developed as a "generation packet" in a mix with other renewables, where a given amount of power is guaranteed regardless whether it comes from a solar/wind or pump-storage generation.

Several countries, such as Indonesia, incentivise hydropower development through legislation by requiring feed-in-tariffs and minimum quotas for purchase of renewable energy.

Policy recommendations designed to maximise the potential from hydropower development in more mature markets include the following:

- Establishing a level playing field on the energy market between hydropower and other technologies.
- Designing the energy market to reflect the true value of firm and flexible energy capacity in different time frames.
- Prevention of double grid fees for pumped storage plants.
- Removing any obstacles to energy trade across borders and strengthen interconnection infrastructure.
- Recognising within the legislation the value of hydropower to maintain the stability and quality of electricity network supply, as an independent aspect from pure power generation (for demand supply).
- Aligning conflicting policy goals and legislation in the field of water management, renewable energy generation, and climate change mitigation and adaptation.
- Leveraging R&D and technology programmes as a contribution to facilitate innovation in hydropower.

Socio-Economic Impacts

Hydropower projects, especially large-scale types, usually tend to be the focus of national policy and public debate. Reasons for this include the high capital investments required, the potential impacts such developments would have on the local environments, the possible displacement of communities from hydropower project sites, and the competing demands between energy, water and land use. While governments generally view hydropower in a favourable light, as they are a means of reducing national emissions, boosting energy security and fostering economic development, hydropower projects can still either enjoy the local support or be met with resistance.

In some cases, public pressure can have a profound effect on the outcome, not only of planned projects, but the entire governing policy on hydropower.

There are, however, many hydropower projects that score high in the socio-economic impacts assessment made by the Hydropower Sustainability Assessment Protocol, demonstrating successful trade-offs between local and national interests. Their equity partnership with IPs could not be bettered in relation to negotiating and reconciling local and national interests. To illustrate this, it was determined that 71% (12 out of 17) of the assessments made via the Sustainability Protocol have scored 5 (highest) on the project benefits topic. Such benefits can be achieved independently of the economic level for the country: Jostedal (Statkraft, Norway) is an excellent developed-country example, and Miel I (ISAGEN, Colombia) is an example applicable to a developing country. Many assessments show very positive results for local employment. Santo Antonio and Chaglla are good examples of this.

It should also be noticed that local and national interests are sometimes directed at reducing and even eliminating the opposing views on a hydropower development, as it is the case of Program Sava in Croatia, for example, where flood management was a major common interest.

The role of governments on hydropower development is to ensure that projects meet acceptable sustainability requirements—economic, social and environmental—and that all negative impacts that may be incurred from the projects are mitigated to the bare minimum. This is of prime importance to developing and emerging economies considering hydropower development, ensuring that the benefits from hydro projects are enjoyed across the country, and especially in areas where the scarce water resources are being exploited.

[...]

An Indian State Leads the Way to Wind Power

John McKenna

John McKenna is a senior writer at Formative Content *and an agenda contributor for the World Economic Forum.*

India's southern state of Tamil Nadu is a world leader when it comes to renewable energy.

Its wind turbines have a combined installed capacity of 7.9 gigawatts (GW). This puts it ahead of many countries regarded as champions of green power.

For example, Sweden is aiming to become one of the first countries to generate 100% of its electricity from renewable sources. But it has a wind-power capacity of 6.7GW, a tenth less than Tamil Nadu.

And Denmark, considered by many as the birthplace of the modern wind energy industry, has a wind-power capacity of 5.5GW.

In fact, figures from the Global Wind Energy Council show that there are only five European nations plus China, the US, Canada and Brazil that had larger installed wind-power capacities than Tamil Nadu in 2017.

Renewables Leader

As well as being India's number one state for wind energy, Tamil Nadu is also top for rooftop solar, and third for overall solar capacity including large-scale solar farms.

Analysis by the Institute For Energy Economics and Financial Analysis (IEEFA) reveals that as a proportion of its overall electricity generating capacity, the Indian state's renewable energy puts it among the best countries and states in the world.

Renewables currently account for 16% of Tamil Nadu's electricity generation, its second largest source of energy after coal.

"This Indian State Produces More Wind Power Than Sweden Or Denmark," by John McKenna, World Economic Forum, February 21, 2018. Reprinted by permission.

More than two thirds of this renewable electricity currently comes from wind turbines, and the IEEFA predicts that Tamil Nadu could nearly double its wind-power capacity to 15GW by 2027.

Meanwhile, solar-power capacity in the state is predicted by the IEEFA to increase more than six-fold over the same period, from today's total solar capacity of 1.7GW to 12GW of solar farms and 1.5GW of rooftop solar panels by 2027.

This rise in renewables is predicted to coincide with a slide in coal's share in Tamil Nadu's electricity mix, from 69% in 2017 to 42% 10 years later.

India On Track to Double Wind Capacity

While Tamil Nadu may currently lead the way on renewables, other areas of India are poised to catch up and even overtake the southern state.

Andhra Pradesh and Rajasthan are already ahead of Tamil Nadu when it comes to solar-power generation, while five Indian states installed more new wind turbines than the 262 megawatts (MW) of capacity added by Tamil Nadu in 2017.

According to the World Resources Institute, the Indian states that added more wind-power capacity than Tamil Nadu last year are: Andhra Pradesh (2.2GW); Gujarat (1.3GW); Karnataka (882MW); Madhya Pradesh (357MW); and Rajasthan (888MW).

Wind energy is India's biggest source of renewable electricity by far, accounting for nearly three times as much generating capacity as solar.

India added 5.5GW of new wind-power capacity in 2017, well ahead of the government's 4GW target for the year.

At current rates of installation, the World Resources Institute predicts that India is well on track to meet the government's target of nearly doubling the country's wind-power capacity to nearly 60GW by 2022.

This would place India, and not just Tamil Nadu, among the elite of the world's wind energy producers.

The Necessity of Government Investment in Clean Energy

Richard W. Caperton

Richard W. Capterton is the Director of National Policy and Partnerships at Opower, where he manages the organization's US policy work with an emphasis on creating policy environments that recognize the benefits of energy efficiency.

Budget deficits drove the conversation in Washington in 2011 with the daily news dominated by government shutdown threats, the "super committee," continuing resolutions, and arcane budgeting practices. Unfortunately, this left Americans convinced that government investments in the future are off the table because of large federal budget deficits that need to be reduced.

Americans were misled. As the Center for American Progress points out, the United States can balance our budget, reduce our long-term debt, and make key investments in our future all at the same time. CAP's plan works toward a more vibrant economy where all Americans are better off and clean energy is an integral part of this future. Best of all, the investments that government needs to make are relatively modest and can be paid for by ending wasteful spending in the same energy sector.

There is no doubt that Americans need clean energy because it's vital to our nation's economic competitiveness, security, and health.

There is also no doubt that government will play an important role in making the transition to clean energy.

Why? Because the federal government always has been—and always will be—a player in energy markets. The federal government has made investments in energy for more than a century, by granting access to resources on public lands, helping build railroads and waterways to transport fuels, building dams to

"Good Government Investments in Renewable Energy," by Richard W. Caperton, Center for American Progress, January 10, 2012. Reprinted by permission.

provide electricity, subsidizing exploration and extraction of fossil fuels, providing financing to electrify rural America, taking on risk in nuclear power, and conducting research and development in virtually all energy sources. There's no reason that Washington should stop making new investments.

Considering the history, government investment has led to amazing developments, including universal access to reliable and affordable electricity, lasting economic development, and industrial growth. This success story alone could justify continued government engagement of vibrant energy markets.

When we consider that investments in clean energy are investments in America's future, it's clear that the smart choice is to make these investments to meet the next generation of energy challenges and to produce a foundation of affordable, reliable, and clean energy alternatives for future waves of investment and opportunity. At the same time we can no longer afford indiscriminate or wasteful subsidies. It is essential that government's investments in energy be fair, effective, and efficient.

This issue brief examines how the government currently invests in renewable energy, when those investments are effective, and how those investments should work in the future.

Energy and the Tax Code

The federal government has a suite of tools at its disposal to make investments, including cash grants, regulatory incentives, tax expenditures, and financing supports. When properly designed and targeted, each of these tools plays an important role.

In the energy sector most government investment happens through the tax code. Indeed, for energy companies that receive federal support, the most important day of the year is Tax Day, when they receive a large amount of their government benefits. In fact, 44 percent of energy spending in 2010 was through the tax system, with the remainder through other tools.

There are both good and bad reasons for this. Both companies and the government have an established system for paying and processing taxes, so providing investments through the tax code provides for efficient delivery of incentives by tapping existing infrastructure and rules. More cynically, however, tax expenditures are an expedient that may be at cross-purposes with good government practice because they are held to different budget standards than direct spending. This means that working through the tax code is less transparent and therefore far easier to pass through Congress with reduced budget scrutiny.

These issues are discussed in detail in the CAP report "Government Spending Undercover: Spending Programs Administered by the IRS" by Lily Batchelder and Eric Toder.

Tax expenditures are government spending programs that deliver subsidies through the tax code via special tax credits, deductions, exclusions, exemptions, and preferential rates. While the actual implementation can be complicated, tax expenditures are economically the same as direct spending both for the government and for beneficiaries. With direct spending, the government brings in tax money and then spends it, while with tax expenditures the government simply reduces the taxes that a company owes. Either way, the company has more money and the federal government has less.

Tax Expenditures Should Be Held Accountable for Achieving Results

The underlying reasons for so much energy spending being done through the tax code are unlikely to change, at least in the short term. Therefore it's important that energy tax expenditures work well. In previous CAP work we've called for regular reviews of all tax expenditures to ensure this spending is effective, efficient, and necessary.

There are some energy tax expenditures that clearly do not meet this standard. Sima Gandhi and I wrote in depth about this issue in "America's Hidden Power Bill," where we described obscure tax credits for the oil-and-gas industry that have existed for more than 80 years and have no demonstrable benefits for Americans.

Such tax breaks simply provide windfall benefits to these mature industries at taxpayer expense. We also discussed several tax credits for clean energy that are much better designed.

This issue brief calls for Congress to take action on some of the most important clean energy tax issues in today's policy and political debates: the production tax credit, the investment tax credit, and the Treasury Cash Grant Program. Each of these can be extended in a way that both leads to powerful incentives for investment in our energy future and represents good tax policy.

Finally, it's important to note that each of the three primary issues is significant for a different reason. Because renewable energy sources have different characteristics they require different treatments within the tax code. Simply extending the production tax credit is not sufficient. Neither is extending the Treasury Cash Grant Program nor improving the investment tax credit. Congress needs to do all of these things. If Congress only takes action on one of these, they will in effect be "picking winners" across technologies.

Congress should instead focus on a comprehensive investment package that creates paths for all technologies so that American businesses will invest in the technologies that make the most sense for our country.

Three Ways to Invest Efficiently and Effectively

Fortunately, we already know some of the best ways for the federal government to make meaningful investments. Through effective and efficient use of the tax code, the government can continue to help drive deployment of the energy technologies that will be critical to our future.

This section describes the three most important tax issues for the government to consider in encouraging the next wave of strategic energy investment in the United States. They are:

- The production tax credit
- The investment tax credit
- The Treasury Cash Grant

Let's look at each in turn.

The Production Tax Credit

The renewable electricity production tax credit, or PTC, is the most critical tax incentive for renewable energy projects using wind, geothermal, biomass, and hydroelectric power technologies, among others. I'll focus on wind here because it's the most prominent, but investment in all of these resources is important.

The PTC is linked to electricity generation from a project. That is, for each kilowatt-hour of electricity produced, the owner of a project gets a tax credit. "Tax credit" means that the owner of the project gets to reduce their tax bill by a certain amount—currently 2.2 cents per kilowatt hour, or kWh—at the end of the year.

Let's look at an example. A typical large wind farm has several dozen turbines that can generate 100 megawatts of electricity. Because the wind conditions are only favorable for part of the year, it won't produce that much power all of the time. Instead, the wind turbines will only spin about 30 percent of the time. This wind farm will generate 262,800,000 kWh each year, which will earn $5,781,600 in tax credits from the PTC.

Let's be clear: This is a $5 million government investment, but it just happens to have gone through the tax code. This tax credit is economically the same as government spending: The government has less money than they would have without the investment, and the project is more profitable. It is also true that the incentive helped stimulate the investment that made both the income and the tax expenditure possible. In short, this investment helped directly create economic activity and growth.

Since its creation in 1993, the government has invested several billion dollars in wind power through the PTC. These have been smart investments. The PTC is intended to incentivize the deployment of energy sources that are more expensive than fossil-fuel sources and whose cost will come down as more of the technology is deployed. This is also known as driving a technology down its cost curve. Since 1980 the cost of wind power has declined by 90 percent.

Declining costs are critical because they allow for more clean energy to be built, which will improve our environment and diversify our power mix. Indeed, the PTC has led to massive amounts of new growth in the wind industry. Since 1993 more than 40 gigawatts of new capacity have come online.

We know this growth is attributable to the PTC.

Since its creation the PTC has only been extended for two years at a time. When it's not in effect, there's virtually zero investment. When it is in effect, investment is tremendous. There are also more formal economic studies suggesting the positive outcome of the PTC: Economist Gilbert Metcalf, for example, finds that "[T]he data suggest that much of the current investment in wind can be explained by the production tax credit for wind." (For more information on how we know the PTC works, see the CAP report, "America's Hidden Power Bill.")

The PTC also has real benefits for American workers. At least 85,000 people work in the wind industry. These workers are spread all across our country and throughout the industry. We have people making turbines, installing them, and operating them, all in good-paying jobs.

Unfortunately, we don't have as many people working in the wind industry as we could. While the wind-manufacturing sector has grown in recent years, it has historically been crippled by the PTC expiring every two years. Manufacturers know that this on-again, off-again cycle for the industry would leave them with virtually no business every other year, so American wind farms use some imported parts.

Indeed, we have more demand for certain turbine parts than we have domestic manufacturing capacity. In particular, US manufacturing capacity is insufficient for gearboxes, generators, bearings, and castings. The lack of consistent policy is clearly contributing to US underinvestment in domestic production of these strategic technologies. Our economic competitors have simultaneously developed robust manufacturing capacity to serve both their growing domestic demand and meet global demand through technology exports.

Over the past three years, however, the United States experienced tremendous growth in wind manufacturing, partly because of the relatively stable PTC, which was most recently extended for four years as part of the 2009 American Recovery and Reinvestment Act, known as the stimulus. In that time new manufacturers set up shop across the country and the composition of domestic parts that each turbine made has steadily increased while our wind energy imports declined. This should be a lesson to Congress: A long-term PTC is more valuable than a short-term extension when we look at the overall impact on jobs and growth.

Instead of allowing the PTC to expire this year, it should be extended for at least four more years to give confidence and stability to investors throughout the supply chain. This doesn't mean, however, that the PTC should be extended indefinitely without review. This is exactly one of the biggest problems with many of the deeply flawed fossil-fuel subsidies. If Congress wants to extend it beyond that timeframe, they should build in a review process to evaluate whether or not the credit should be adjusted in any way.

Congress should review the size of the credit and review whether or not it should be linked to inflation. Ultimately as the industry matures and markets expand, the PTC—like other subsidies that have done their work and grown strong domestic industries—should be allowed to sunset, taking taxpayers off the hook for payments.

The Investment Tax Credit

While the production tax credit primarily benefits wind, the solar industry is the primary beneficiary of the investment tax credit, or ITC. The ITC works a little differently, in a way that makes more economic sense for the type of capital investment required for developing solar energy projects. Instead of the tax credit being spread over 10 years and only awarded as energy is produced, renewable energy developers get an upfront tax credit based on the initial investment in the project. For solar power the credit is worth 30 percent of the initial investment.

So if a building owner spends $6 million to put a 1 megawatt solar energy system on a building's rooftop, the building owner is then awarded a $1.8 million tax credit—but the owner is not allowed to claim any other tax credits over the life of the project.

The upfront, one-time nature of the ITC has some real benefits for solar power. First, solar is a more expensive technology to initially install, so investors have a special need for the investment-based incentive. Second, solar is a younger industry than wind, and the technology isn't quite as proven over the long term. This means that future energy production is slightly less certain with solar power than with wind power, so a production-based incentive would be less valuable.

Just like the PTC, the ITC has been a tremendous success. The solar industry has experienced extremely impressive cost improvements.

Not surprisingly, as costs fall and demand rises, the solar industry now employs more than 100,000 people, up from 20,000 just five years ago.

The ITC was extended until 2016 as part of the stimulus bill. The extension provided very valuable certainty to the solar market, but when it expires Congress should also review the size and effectiveness of this credit.

The Treasury Cash Grant in Lieu of Tax Credits

Despite their incredible successes, the PTC and ITC aren't perfect, and they don't provide a complete offering to meet the full range of project-financing needs faced in the emerging renewable energy market. The biggest problem is that most renewable energy projects are structured in such a way that they don't earn profits for the first several years of the project's life. The developer only owes taxes on profits (not revenues), so they may not owe any taxes for years after building the project.

At the same time, tax credits are used to reduce the amount of taxes owed. Thus, if the developer doesn't owe any taxes, the associated credits are worthless. This is a structural limitation of using the tax code to support strategically valuable public investments.

Traditionally, project developers have worked around this problem by bringing in so-called "tax equity investors." These investors—typically large financial institutions— essentially buy the tax credits from a project. This cash from the tax equity investor is extremely valuable and allows developers to monetize the tax benefits without actually owing taxes.

This system worked fairly well before the financial crisis. There was more than $6 billion in tax equity available in 2007. The pool of tax equity capital shrank dramatically, though, when large financial institutions no longer owed taxes, as they lost money in 2008 and 2009.

This shortfall was fixed with something called the Treasury Cash Grant Program. This program, also known as the Section 1603 program because of where it's included in the stimulus bill, does two things:

- It makes the PTC-eligible technologies also eligible for the ITC.
- It allows developers to get a cash grant instead of the ITC.

This means that all renewable developers are able to get a cash grant from the Treasury Department for 30 percent of the initial investment in their project. This solved the tax equity market shortfall problem, and allowed renewable investments to continue. Instead of shrinking, the wind and solar industries grew during the recent recession, largely because the Section 1603 program helped with financing.

Unfortunately, this program drew to a close at the end of 2011. After creating the program in 2009, Congress extended it for one year at the end of 2010. Now they should extend the program for at least one more year, and ideally change it to run concurrently with the underlying PTC and ITC, always matching their expiration dates. This is especially important because there's not expected to be enough tax equity available to meet the demand. In 2011 the US Partnership for Renewable Energy Finance estimated that there was a total of $7.5 billion available through tax equity and the Treasury Cash Grant. They project that there will only be $3.6 billion in tax equity available in 2012, which is far less than recent history suggests will be needed.

The cash grant program makes the PTC and ITC more effective, more efficient, and more transparent. It makes absolutely no sense to have this beneficial program on a different schedule than the tax credits it improves.

In addition to overcoming a simple shortfall in investment capital from the tax equity market, the cash grant program has several benefits that make it superior to a tax credit.

First, the cash grant is more economically efficient. In a best-case scenario, the tax equity investor is going to buy tax credits at a slight discount (it makes no sense to pay full price because then there's no possible profit for the investor). In real life, however, there's evidence that tax equity investors buy tax credits at a much deeper discount. The Bipartisan Policy Center finds that even though a tax credit and cash grant may have the same face value to the government, the tax credit is only half as valuable as the cash grant to the project developer and thus is dramatically less effective at producing clean energy outcomes.

Second, the cash grant is much more transparent. When a developer claims the ITC, all they do is check a box and write in a number on a tax form. When they claim the cash grant, however, they submit much more information, such as details on the project and the number of jobs that will be created with the investment. And while tax information is strictly confidential, the Treasury publishes a list of every project that has received a Section 1603 cash grant.

If Congress does choose to extend the cash grant program to always match the PTC and ITC extensions, thus making this public spending more efficient for taxpayers, they should also evaluate the size of the tax credits. The overwhelming popularity and the evidence of the cash grant's economic efficiency seem to indicate that the ITC could be made smaller if it is always offered as a cash grant.

Expanding the Investment Tax Credit for Offshore Wind

In addition to the three key policies described above, there is a fourth way that the tax code could be improved to boost renewable energy. For many years the technologies eligible for the PTC and ITC have remained unchanged. But there's no reason that new developments in renewable energy technology shouldn't be accounted for with modifications to the tax code. Most importantly Congress should place technologies within the PTC or ITC (or both) depending on the unique characteristics of each technology and their specific capital investment needs.

The offshore wind industry is poised to take off in the waters off of America's East Coast. Unfortunately, as Michael Conathan and I wrote in "Clean Energy from America's Oceans," "More than 40,000 megawatts of offshore wind energy capacity have been permitted around the globe, yet the United States accounts for barely 1 percent of that, and we have yet to generate our first watt of electricity from this abundant, carbon-free source of power."

There's no shortage of interest in building offshore wind farms and several projects are moving forward with permitting and siting. The right government investment can provide critical support for leveraging private capital investment in these projects to accelerate the growth of this new American industry.

In many ways, offshore wind looks more like solar than it looks like onshore wind. For instance, the technology has extremely high upfront costs. These are expected to rapidly decline over time, but they are currently a significant barrier to investors entering this market.

Further, the offshore wind technology is largely unknown and unproven in the eyes of American investors and returns are therefore discounted in the capital market. Because the future production from an offshore wind farm is less certain than with onshore wind, the value of the production tax credit is also unpredictable.

Congress should address this issue by making offshore wind temporarily eligible for the ITC, which better suits this emerging industry. As the industry grows and more closely resembles onshore wind, the technology should shift back to the PTC.

Conclusion

Clean, renewable energy is a bright spot in the US economy. This industry is a success story that has resulted in job creation, scientific innovation, cleaner air, and a stronger manufacturing sector.

Yet this is still a young industry and it still needs significant public investment. Importantly, this investment should be structured in a way that supports the entire industry in an efficient, cost-effective manner. When the government invests in clean energy, they need to match the tools available to the specific technologies and businesses that they're supporting.

In this issue brief we have explained why the production tax credit should be extended. This is the fundamental tool that the government uses to invest in renewable energy, and it has been a tremendous success. But extending the PTC is not sufficient to support the whole industry.

Other technologies require an investment tax credit, which can be made more effective when issued as a cash grant, as in the Section 1603 Treasury Cash Grant Program.

Finally, there are new types of renewable energy that are not properly treated in existing law. Offshore wind power is much better suited to the ITC than the PTC, and Congress acknowledged this by making offshore wind specifically eligible for the ITC.

This strategy of strong investment in renewable energy, with the investment channeled through a mix of tools, will make America a better place. Congress should start 2012 by making this happen.

The Cost of Clean Energy for Developing Countries

Tucker Davey

Tucker Davey is a Boston College graduate with a degree in political science, philosophy, and Hispanic studies. Davey primarily examines climate change and artificial intelligence, and he is particularly interested in the relationship between technology and society and the psychology of existential risks.

Developing countries currently cannot sustain themselves, let alone grow, without relying heavily on fossil fuels. Global warming typically takes a back seat to feeding, housing, and employing these countries' citizens. Yet the weather fluctuations and consequences of climate change are already impacting food growth in many of these countries. Is there a solution?

Developing Countries Need Fossil Fuels

Fossil fuels are still the cheapest, most reliable energy resources available. When a developing country wants to build a functional economic system and end rampant poverty, it turns to fossil fuels.

India, for example, is home to one-third of the world's 1.2 billion citizens living in poverty. That's 400 million people in one country without sufficient food or shelter (for comparison, the entire US population is roughly 323 million people). India hopes to transition to renewable energy as its economy grows, but the investment needed to meet its renewable energy goals "is equivalent to over four times the country's annual defense spending, and over ten times the country's annual spending on health and education."

Unless something changes, developing countries like India cannot fight climate change *and* provide for their citizens. In fact, developing countries will only accelerate global warming as their

"Developing Countries Can't Afford Climate Change," by Tucker Davey, Future of Life Institute, August 5, 2016. Reprinted by permission.

economies grow because they cannot afford alternatives. Wealthy countries cannot afford to ignore the impact of these growing, developing countries.

The Link Between Economic Growth and CO_2

According to a World Bank report, "poor and middle-income countries already account for just over half of total carbon emissions." And this percentage will only rise as developing countries grow. Achieving a global society in which all citizens earn a living wage and climate catastrophe is averted requires breaking the link between economic growth and increasing carbon emissions in developing countries.

Today, most developing countries that *decrease their poverty rates also have increased rates of carbon emissions.* In East Asia and the Pacific, the number of people living in extreme poverty declined from 1.1 billion to 161 million between 1981 and 2011—an 85% decrease. In this same time period, the amount of carbon dioxide per capita rose from 2.1 tons per capita to 5.9 tons per capita—a 185% increase.

South Asia saw similar changes during this time frame. As the number of people living in extreme poverty decreased by 30%, the amount of carbon dioxide increased by 204%.

In Sub-Saharan Africa, the number of people living in poverty *increased* by 98% in this thirty-year span, while carbon dioxide per capita *decreased* by 17%. Given the current energy situation, if sub-Saharan Africans are to escape extreme poverty, they will have to increase their carbon use—unless developed countries step in to offer clean alternatives.

Carbon Emissions Rate Vs. Total

Many wealthier countries have been researching alternative forms of energy for decades. And that work may be starting to pay off.

New data shows that, since the year 2000, 21 developed countries have reduced annual greenhouse gas emissions while simultaneously growing their economies. Moreover, this isn't all related to a drop in the industrial sector. Uzbekistan, Bulgaria, Switzerland, and the Czech Republic demonstrated that countries do not need to shrink their industrial sectors to break the link between economic growth and increased greenhouse gas emissions.

Most importantly, global carbon emissions stalled from 2014 to 2015 as the global economy grew.

But is this rate of global decoupling fast enough to keep the planet from warming another two degrees Celsius? When emissions stall at 32.1 billion metric tons for two years, that's still 64.2 billion metric tons of carbon being pumped into the atmosphere over two years.

The carbon emissions *rate* might fall, but the *total* continues to grow enormously. A sharp decline in carbon emissions is necessary to keep the planet at a safe global temperature. At the 2015 Paris Climate Conference, the United Nations concluded that in order to keep global temperatures from rising another two degrees Celsius, global carbon emissions "must fall to net zero in the second half of the century."

In order to encourage this, the Paris agreement included measures to ensure that wealthy countries finance developing countries "with respect to both mitigation and adaptation." For mitigation, countries are expected to abide by their pledges to reduce emissions and use more renewable energy, and for adaptation, the deal sets a global goal for "enhancing adaptive capacity, strengthening resilience and reducing vulnerability to climate change."

Incentivizing R&D

One way wealthy countries can benefit both themselves and developing countries is through research and development. As wealthier countries develop cheaper forms of alternative energy, developing countries can take advantage of the new technologies. Wealthy countries can also help subsidize renewable energy for countries dealing with higher rates of poverty.

Yet, as of 2014, wealthy countries had invested very little in this process, providing only 0.2% of developing countries' GDP for adaptation and mitigation. Moreover, a 2015 paper from the IMF revealed that while we spend $100 billion per year subsidizing renewable energy, we spend an estimated $5.3 trillion subsidizing fossil fuels. This fossil fuel subsidy includes "the uncompensated costs of air pollution, congestion and global warming."

Such a huge disparity indicates that wealthy countries either need stronger incentives or stronger legal obligations to shift this fossil fuel money towards renewable energy. The Paris agreement intends to strengthen legal obligations, but its language is vague, and it lacks details that would ensure wealthy countries follow through with their responsibilities.

However, despite the shortcomings of legal obligations, monetary incentives do exist. India, for example, wants to vastly increase its solar power capacity to address this global threat. They need $100 billion to fund this expansion, which could spell a huge opportunity for US banks, according to Raymond Vickery, an expert on US-India economic ties. This would be a boon for the US economy, and it would set an important precedent for other wealthy countries to assist and invest in developing countries.

However, global leaders need to move quickly. The effects of global warming already threaten the world and the economies of developing countries, especially India.

Global Impact of Climate Change

India relies on the monsoon cycle to water crops and maintain its "nearly $370 billion agricultural sector and hundreds of millions of jobs." Yet as the Indian Ocean has warmed, the monsoon cycle has become unreliable, resulting in massive droughts and dying crops.

Across the globe, scientists expect developing countries such as India to be hit hardest by rising temperatures and changes in rainfall. Furthermore, these countries with limited financial resources and weak infrastructure will struggle to adapt and sustain their economic growth in the face of changing climate. Nicholas

Stern predicts that a two-degree rise in temperature would cost about 1% of world GDP. But the World Bank estimates that it would cost India 5% of their GDP.

Moreover, changes such as global warming act as "threat multipliers" because they increase the likelihood of other existential threats. In India, increased carbon dioxide emissions have contributed to warmer temperatures, which have triggered extensive droughts and increased poverty. But the problems don't end here. Higher levels of hunger and poverty can magnify political tensions, potentially leading to conflict and even nuclear war. India and Pakistan both have nuclear weapons—if drought expands and cripples their economies, violence can more easily erupt.

Alternatively, wealthy nations could capitalize on investment opportunities in developing countries. In doing so, their own economies will benefit while simultaneously aiding the effort to reach net zero carbon emissions.

Global warming is, by definition, a global crisis. Mitigating this threat will require global cooperation and global solutions.

Federal Investment in Clean Energy Is Too High

Megan Nicholson and Matthew Stepp

Megan Nicholson served as a policy analyst and Matthew Stepp was Director of the Center for Clean Energy Innovation at the Information Technology & Innovation Foundation. Nicholson specialized in clean energy policy and the role of the Department of Defense in the energy innovation system, while Stepp researched and analyzed issues related to clean energy policy.

The United States has failed to create a comprehensive energy policy that provides robust and consistent support for innovation. Although the Recovery and Reinvestment Act of 2009 stimulated public investments in energy innovation, many of these programs and incentives have since expired or concluded, leaving the energy innovation ecosystem underfunded and skewed towards supporting deployment incentives over technology R&D, demonstration, and manufacturing.

[…]

Defining the Energy Innovation Ecosystem

A pervasive problem persists in the clean energy policy debate: innovation policy is often misrepresented as only research, or largely ignored by advocates to support rigid economic doctrines or policy goals that divert attention from addressing climate change (e.g. short-term green job creation). This type of clean energy policy fundamentalism de-emphasizes the need for cheap, new, clean energy technologies and muddles innovation's foundational role in US clean energy policy. By extension, the process inhibits

"Breaking Down Federal Investments in Clean Energy," by Megan Nicholson and Matthew Stepp, Information Technology and Innovation Foundation, March 2013. Reprinted by permission.

America's abilities to drastically cut carbon emissions as quickly as possible.

Providing clarity on what characterizes clean energy innovation policy is critically important to understanding the components of a healthy innovation ecosystem. The first step towards improving the nation's energy innovation system is defining the individual but linked stages of technology innovation.

Basic Science

Basic energy science is fundamental scientific research in fields like chemistry, biology, and physics that often don't have an obvious commercial outcome but could enable a suite of energy solutions. The National Science Foundation invested $43 million in basic energy science projects through university grants in FY2013 covering a wide gamut of science issues potentially related to energy, such as developing fundamentally new ways to grow nano-crystals which could have significant impact for fuel cells and biomedical technologies. The Department of Energy Office of Science, on the other hand, conducts basic energy research in high-energy physics, nuclear energy, super-computing and chemistry both through University grants, but also through the National Laboratory system. Projects include fundamental research in plasma technology, quantum physics, and the creation of new materials and biochemistries, to name a few.

Research and Development

As basic science progresses in the lab and potential uses and outcomes become more apparent, additional research and development (R&D) is necessary. R&D is specific research that addresses explicit technological needs through creating proof-of-concept prototypes. In many ways this research is still early-stage, but often with more focused purpose and goals. For instance, the Department of Agriculture invests in several different feedstock and conversion process R&D projects in order to target the most cost-effective and efficient combination for creating next-generation biofuels ($11 million in FY2011), while the Department of Transportation's NextGen Aircraft Technologies program supports the development of alternative jet fuels and low-carbon aviation systems and technologies through early-stage prototyping ($20.1 million in FY2011).

DOE's Advanced Research Projects Agency–Energy (ARPA-E) offers the most comprehensive picture of laudable public R&D investments; the agency funds early- stage research through prototyping of potentially "transformative" energy technologies that would otherwise be too risky for private investors. ARPA-E was initially funded by the Recovery Act, and was appropriated $143 million in FY2011 and $243 million in FY2012.

Technology Demonstration

Demonstration projects offer the opportunity to show users the practical utility of a new technology, while enabling researchers to collect data on its technical and economic characteristics under realistic conditions and address any remaining research gaps. Because of the capital-intensive nature of energy technologies, demonstration projects are often expensive and are underfunded by the private sector, however despite the high cost of these projects, they are highly valuable because they offer increased access to information to all stakeholders. In fact, for many energy technologies like utility-scale solar, wind, and carbon capture projects, demonstrating its first-of-kind commercial potential is absolutely necessary to gain private sector support for the technology.

Examples of this kind of investment include the American Recovery and Reinvestment Act (ARRA) investment of $685 million in the demonstration of competitively selected, large-scale grid projects to measure performance and cost in a realistic market. The Pacific Northwest Division Smart Grid Demonstration Project installed industrial smart metering, electricity storage technologies, and direct load control devices to distribute power to more than 60,000 customers across five states to validate technology readiness and assess costs and benefits of the enhanced grid system. DOD also supports projects demonstrating advancements in energy technology in pursuit of achieving greater operational capabilities—their Great Green Fleet project equips tanks and other combat vehicles with a variety of energy technologies including fuel cell engines and energy storage and power electronics systems. Investment in the suite of projects contributing to the Great Green Fleet demonstration totaled about $82 million in FY2012.

Siting and Permitting

Support for siting and permitting offers technical and regulatory assistance for planning and management within current policies. Projects focused on siting and permitting often conduct market research for technology commercialization prior to the deployment stage; this kind of research can be as procedural as Department of Commerce research on coastal and marine spatial planning for potential offshore wind locations (which cost $1.5 million in FY2011) or as objective as DOE's market transformation and systems integration programs within the Office of Energy Efficiency and Renewable Energy (EERE) (which totaled $31 million in FY2011) that research other non-hardware barriers to technology commercialization such as potential regional or industry collaborations, addressing concerns for the wide-spread adoption of emerging energy technologies.

Technology Deployment

Even after a technology has been demonstrated at full-scale, financing for its full commercialization may not be easily attained because of the nature of the energy industry and the low (often subsidized) cost of fossil fuels. Technology deployment investments can help create economies of scale for technologies by creating an initial customer base, promoting information sharing about the technology, allowing producers to streamline manufacturing processes, and permitting installers to lower costs. Deployment support can directly apply to either commercial "off-the-shelf" technologies that are readily available in the marketplace, or emerging technologies that are not widely available in commercial markets.

The Department of the Treasury is in charge of administering a number of deployment programs through tax incentives that support both clean and conventional energy technologies—the much-discussed Energy Production Tax Credit is one such incentive available to producers of clean energy technologies (wind, solar, biomass, etc.) that provides a subsidy to any eligible clean energy project. In a parallel way the Department of Interior supports the deployment of energy technologies through the department-wide New Energy Frontier initiative, which funds the deployment of renewable and conventional energy on public lands.

Government Procurement

An additional way that public investments can promote the innovation of clean energy technologies is through acquisition of technologies by the federal government acquiring technologies. Like deployment incentives, government procurement can create early markets for emerging technologies that are too risky for commercial markets, but show future promise. For example, early government purchasing of the microchip allowed produces to quickly lower costs and eventually take the product to market, revolutionizing the electronic industry. In energy, General Services Administration (GSA) and DOD procurement are the top agencies capable of creating early markets for breakthrough technologies. ITIF's recent report, *Lean, Mean, and Green II: Assessing DOD Investments in Clean Energy Innovation* suggested that DOD's operational energy challenges drove the department to invest $540 million in FY2012 in the procurement of energy technologies, and about 70 percent of this investment was for acquiring emerging technologies. DOD's procurement process provides the demand and the capital for the production of these emerging technologies, which in turn offers potential for bringing the technologies to commercial markets.

Manufacturing

The future of a competitive clean energy industry in the United States hinges on significant investments in clean energy technology manufacturing. While the previous innovation phases are integral in developing advanced technologies, without a significant manufacturing sector the country continues to rely on the manufacturing capacities of other countries, losing its competitive advantage as an innovator of breakthrough energy solutions. The Section 48C Advanced Energy Manufacturing Tax Credit, for example, awarded funds to energy producers to update or build facilities for the manufacture of advanced wind, solar, geothermal, and other renewable energy technologies.

Improving the pathway towards competitive clean energy in the United States lies in improving the quality of our innovation system—but these improvements can only begin with a full understanding of the innovation ecosystem itself. Defining energy innovation at this level of detail exposes the features of a working ecosystem more thoroughly, and defining public investments according to these phases can uncover white spaces that require additional funding, areas of policy weakness, or areas where there may be over-funding.

Trends in Public Investments in Clean Energy Innovation

Clean energy innovation encompasses more than any one policy, whether it is R&D, tax incentives, regulation, or an economy-wide carbon price. Well-designed public investments impact the entire energy innovation ecosystem and fill gaps in next-generation technology development and deployment.

In the case of federal investments in energy innovation since FY2009, technology development captures all investments in basic science, research and development, demonstration; technology deployment investments facilitate the installation and procurement of clean energy technologies in commercial markets, along with supporting investments in siting and permitting and training and education.

During the past four years, the balance between development and deployment has evolved dramatically, driven in part by increased procurement of emerging and commercial off-the-shelf energy technologies by the Department of Defense, as well as expanded deployment initiatives and tax incentives through the Department of Energy and the US Treasury Department. Between 2009 and 2011, investment in deployment and procurement of clean energy technologies nearly quadrupled, while investment in R&D and demonstration projects remained relatively steady or declined. All told, technology deployment and procurement now captures about 63.8 percent of the clean energy innovation budget, while technology development captures 36.1 percent.

Loan guarantee programs also contributed to the demonstration and deployment of clean energy technologies during the last four years and through the Recovery Act by providing temporary financing for projects and technological systems close to commercialization. The impacts of these investments on the development of technologies has high value, but the cost to the government to back loan guarantees is only a fraction of the actual loan amount. Because of this distinction from direct government spending, loan guarantees are not counted in this section. Costs and impacts of loan guarantees are explained in further detail in the subsequent sections on demonstration projects and deployment incentives.

The impact of significant investments in clean energy innovation through the American Recovery and Reinvestment Act (ARRA) cannot be overstated. The Recovery Act directly increased federal funding of research and demonstration projects through a series of new programs and initiatives, and also established many tax incentives for the adoption of energy efficiency and renewable energy technologies that were extended into FY2012. While some critics accuse the Recovery Act of coming up short in its effort to reverse the effects of the Great Recession on the American economy, it super-charged energy innovation with public investments in new programs, and created new opportunities for funding of advanced energy R&D through ARPA-E.

Distributing ARRA funds equally between FY2009 and FY2010 (the fiscal years during which most of the Recovery Act funds were distributed) suggests that total investment in clean energy has fallen nearly $8 billion since FY2010—a significant decline by any standard. But understanding the characteristics of the decline reveals troubling evidence of the stagnation of policy development at the federal level.

In real terms, funding for deployment incentives declined by over $6 billion, but as a percentage of total clean energy innovation investment, deployment incentives only declined slightly, from 66 percent of total funding to 59 percent between FY2010 and FY2012. In comparison, funding for demonstration projects was decimated over the same period, falling from 6 percent of total spending in FY2011 to just 0.2 percent in FY2012 (a 97 percent decrease).

The significant decline of federal support for demonstration projects post-Recovery Act is a symptom of the lack of dedicated US technology demonstration policy—a weakness affecting the productivity of the country's innovation ecosystem.

As previously argued by ITIF and the Breakthrough Institute, demonstration projects are characteristically often very capital-intensive, but also serve as the key to driving a technology from the research stage to market. First-of kind investments in emerging clean energy projects often serve as an educational exercise for technology producers, manufacturers, and consumers alike, consequently playing an integral role in the bridging of the commercialization valley of death that can limit development of (especially energy) technologies from finding a place in commercial markets alongside cheap, heavily subsidized conventional energy.

In lieu of expiring Recovery Act investments, the United States clean energy innovation ecosystem shows signs of being hollowed out. Strong industry focus sustains some deployment incentives like the Production Tax Credit, but overall investments continue to decline. Demonstration projects that prepare technologies for market acceptance and integration have been shouldered. And technology development investments, especially R&D investments, remain stagnate. Ultimately, the current federal clean energy innovation budget is not only underfunded, but is also less diversified across innovations phases, potentially resulting in significant barriers to next-generation energy innovation.

The next sections identify the contributing sources of this decline by examining investment trends within the demonstration, deployment, and manufacturing innovation stages.

[...]

Deep Dive into Deployment Incentives

For the last few years, the lion's share of debate on US clean energy policy has focused on encouraging deployment—or large-scale construction and installation—of low-carbon technologies. By significantly deploying clean energy technologies, supporters say, the United States can encourage integration of emerging technologies in an energy market dominated by entrenched fossil fuel interests, spur cost-cutting economies of scale, and get started on lowering greenhouse gas emissions in the process. However, others argue that there is a necessity to designing well-constructed deployment incentives aimed at directly spurring innovation to address climate change.

Typology of Deployment Policies

Federal clean energy deployment incentives can be made available through grants and other annually appropriated programs. For instance, the State and Tribal Energy Programs at the Department of Energy (DOE) deploy building efficiency and renewable energy technologies within communities. The New Energy Frontier initiative at the Department of the Interior (DOI) deploys renewable and energy efficiency technologies on federal lands. While direct spending on deployment incentives of this type is typically minor in comparison to other direct spending programs, the Recovery Act significantly increased direct spending for deployment by funding the Advanced Battery Manufacturing Grants program, which awarded funding to projects that accelerated the manufacture and deployment of batteries for electric vehicles.

More commonly, federal deployment incentives are driven by consumer and corporate tax credits, and through loan programs that help finance construction of large-scale technology installations. Investment in deployment programs was highest in FY2011 at $22.3 billion because of large tax and loan guarantee expenditures. In fact, the most significant deployment investment nearly every year between FY2009-2012 came from tax expenditures, which accounted for 80 percent of total investment in FY2010, 51 percent in FY2011, and 87 percent in FY2012.

Tax expenditures support a multitude of technology priorities including the production of low-carbon electricity, the installation of energy efficiency and renewable energy retrofits on homes and commercial buildings, and the production of low-carbon fuels. Many of the loan guarantee expenditures awarded during FY2011 were from the Recovery Act's Title XVII Section 1705 Loan Program, which supported deployment of mainly solar and wind technologies.

Commercial and Emerging Technologies

An important distinction often overlooked in the clean energy deployment policy debate is whether public investment supports existing or emerging technologies. Federal deployment investments are historically directed at supporting commercial off-the-shelf technologies (i.e. technologies that are readily available in commercial markets), rather than emerging technologies (i.e. nascent technologies being introduced to commercial markets for the first time), with loan guarantees and tax incentives.

This difference is particularly important in determining whether deployment policies are linked to research investments and provide a strong pipeline for emerging technologies to reach market. Today, most clean energy technologies are not cost- and performance- competitive compared to conventional energy technologies. By deploying these technologies at a larger-scale, the nation is focusing its resources on making clean energy competitive by subsidizing the cost to producers and consumers, with the hope that (1) economies of scale will drive costs below that of fossil fuels and allow subsidies to lapse and (2) by providing existing clean energy technologies a niche footprint in the market, deployment policies are providing an opening for emerging technologies close to the commercialization phase.

Creating an Innovation-Centric National Deployment Policy
Deployment incentives are an integral part of the innovation ecosystem because they help reduce costs, eliminate information and infrastructure barriers to achieving market introduction, and create new markets for next-generation technologies. Unfortunately the nation's current system of subsidization and financing is chiefly focused on deploying mature technologies, instead of providing a direct pipeline for emerging technologies to reach market. Implementing deployment tools that only support the most mature technology options can potentially help pull emerging technologies into the market. In fact, wind turbine companies constructing wind fields because of the Production Tax Credit are also now able to work with researchers, such as those the National Renewable Energy Laboratory, on next-generation turbine designs. But the connection between research and market for other industries like solar and battery storage is not so clear.

Well-structured deployment policies with innovation in mind – such as those that leverage performance standards to foster companies to innovate, or those that spur regional collaborations that tie research with deployment options – are needed to move these industries to competitiveness as quickly as possible. Even the wind industry could better utilize incentives to ensure that the most innovative wind turbines, and not just the most mature, are installed using public investment.

Public investments in deploying emerging technologies are at an all-time low; an innovation ecosystem absent this investment stifles technological change and directly impacts America's response to climate change. Emerging technologies are what ultimately will drive carbon emissions to zero as quickly as possible by providing low- cost, high-performance alternatives to fossil fuels. The imperative to accelerate the development and deployment of these technologies is quickly growing. In other words, not only must we increase public investment in deployment, we must also ensure complementary reforms to the policies themselves to emphasize support for emerging technologies in the context of improving our innovation ecosystem. This is a taller task for sure, but one that is desperately needed if we are to meet our climate goals.

The Clean Energy Manufacturing Sector

There is an eminent need for supporting a well-developed and funded clean energy manufacturing sector as part of a robust innovation ecosystem. The feedback loops between manufacturing and research are explicitly linked.21 Even with all the R&D, demonstration, and deployment of clean energy, the United States could lose its competitive advantage over production resulting in the industry (and future innovation) to move overseas without strong policy support for advanced manufacturing. But like many other parts of America's energy innovation budget, support for advanced manufacturing is rapidly declining.

Investment in clean energy manufacturing has fallen from nearly $9 billion to only $700 million between FY2009 and FY2012, or a 92 percent decrease. Direct spending in FY2009 and FY2010 was directly supported by the distribution of the Recovery Act's 48 advanced battery manufacturing grants, which the Department of Energy awarded to a range of electric-drive, battery component, and battery recycling facilities. The grants were all devoted to accelerating the development of US battery and electric vehicle manufacturing.

Absent these grants, EERE's Advanced Manufacturing Office (formerly the Industrial Technologies Program) accounted for all direct spending in FY2011 and FY2012, supporting investments in furthering next generation manufacturing processes and materials, nano-manufacturing projects, and development and training projects to enhance the technical skills and energy-consciousness of America's workforce. In FY2012 the AMO appropriations was more than double that of FY2011. The office invested six times more in energy-intensive process R&D this past fiscal year, and also funded the Critical Materials Hub, which was established to confront projected supply chain disruptions to clean energy manufacturing.

A significant piece of clean energy manufacturing support ($5.9 billion) came from a loan guarantee distributed in FY2009 to the Ford Motor Company through the Advanced Technologies Vehicle Manufacturing Loan Program. The loan guarantee was used to upgrade factories and increase fuel efficiency in commercially-popular vehicles. The program made three other guarantees to electric vehicle manufacturers in FY2010, which amounted to $2.4 billion.

When separated from fiscal year appropriations, Recovery Act funds are accountable for a significant portion of investment in manufacturing during the last four years, both because of the loan guarantee program mentioned previously, and because of the advanced battery manufacturing grants for producers of electric vehicle batteries and components ($2.4 billion). The third major piece of clean energy manufacturing investment was the Section 48(c) Advanced Energy Manufacturing Tax Credit ($2.3 billion), which supported creation and updating of manufacturing facilities for renewable energy technology producers by allowing producers up to a 30 percent tax credit.

The Administration has tried repeatedly to extend the 48(c) tax credit, but has been unsuccessful to date. Combined, these three manufacturing policies accounted for 82 percent of total US manufacturing investment since 2009. While they may individually have long-lasting impacts, intermittent funding opportunities like these encourage investment in the short-term. Significant growth in the clean energy manufacturing sector will only be stimulated by a strong policy commitment over time.

While clean energy manufacturing is not often characterized as part of the energy innovation ecosystem, a strong manufacturing sector acts as an integral vehicle for producing clean energy technologies at economies of scale to drive down costs as well as acting as a key source for future research. America's declining support for manufacturing is troubling, but new ideas are being worked on, though funding concerns still continue.

Strong support for a manufacturing sector in the United States is not only necessary to develop and deploy cost-effective clean energy technologies, it is also significant to ensuring the nation's manufacturing competitiveness on the global scale. ITIF has written extensively (and recently) on why the administration's National Network for Manufacturing Innovation (NNMI) plan should be put to action.22 While the health of US manufacturing has planed off dramatically during the past decade, an NNMI could coordinate a recovery that leads to increases in productivity and job growth, and the recovery of America's innovation ecosystem. To grow the clean energy economy and reduce carbon emissions in the in the United States, the importance of the manufacturing sector must not be forgotten.

Conclusion

Public investments in innovation are essential to advancing technologies from early- stage research through commercialization. This principle, proven by historical evidence, is especially important for the development of clean energy technologies because the process is more capital intensive, and technologies must compete within a current energy system running on cheap fossil fuels. Recognition of the need for public investments in support of energy innovation on its own, however, is not enough. Knowing where to direct those investments – for basic science, R&D, demonstration, deployment, and manufacturing of clean energy technologies – is even more significant.

Appreciating the state of the US clean energy innovation ecosystem is the first step in recognizing ways to improve it. The analysis presented here suggests that in many ways the American Recovery and Reinvestment Act of 2009 elevated public investments in clean energy innovation to record levels. Unfortunately most of these investments were short-lived. Since the expiration of Recovery Act programs and tax credits supporting demonstration and manufacturing of clean energy technologies, in addition to continued budget cuts, the energy innovation ecosystem has been hollowed out.

Constructing a successful and enduring energy innovation ecosystem requires significant public investment, substantial policy commitment to the development of clean energy technologies, and considerable, smart policy options that can continue to drive energy innovation forward. A comprehensive strategy for meeting these challenges in the future is incomplete without a thorough understanding of current policy.

Organizations to Contact

The editors have compiled the following list of organizations concerned with the issues debated in this book. The descriptions are derived from materials provided by the organizations. All have publications or information available for interested readers. This list was compiled on the date of publication of the present volume; the information provided here may change. Be aware that many organizations take several weeks or longer to respond to inquiries, so allow as much time as possible.

American Council on Renewable Energy
1600 K Street NW, Suite 650
Washington, DC 20006
phone: (202) 393-0001
email: info@acore.org
website: acore.org

Founded in 2001, the American Council on Renewable Energy (ACORE) is a 501 (c)(3) national nonprofit organization that unites finance, policy, and technology to accelerate the transition to a renewable energy economy. ACORE accomplishes much of its work by convening leaders across key constituencies, facilitating partnerships, educating senior officials on important policies, publishing research and analysis on pressing issues, and undertaking strategic outreach on the policies and financial structures essential to renewable energy growth.

Center for Clean Energy Innovation at the Information Technology & Innovation Foundation (ITIF)
1101 K St. NW #610
Washington, DC 20005
phone: (202) 524-4393
email: mail@itif.org
website: itif.org

Founded in 2006, ITIF is an independent 501(c)(3) nonprofit, nonpartisan research and educational institute—a think tank—whose mission is to formulate, evaluate, and promote policy solutions that accelerate innovation and boost productivity to spur growth, opportunity, and progress. ITIF's goal is to provide policy makers around the world with high-quality information, analysis, and recommendations they can trust. To that end, ITIF adheres to a high standard of research integrity with an internal code of ethics grounded in the core values of analytical rigor, policy pragmatism, and independence from external direction or bias.

Clean Energy Group
50 State St., Suite 1
Montpelier, VT 05602
phone: (802) 223-2554
email: info@cleanegroup.org
website: cleanegroup.org

Clean Energy Group is a leading national nonprofit advocacy organization working on innovative policy, technology, and finance programs in the areas of clean energy and climate change. They promote effective clean energy policies, develop low-carbon technology innovation strategies, and work on new financial tools to advance clean energy markets. Clean Energy Group assists states in creating and implementing innovative practices and public funding programs for clean energy project deployment; creates networks of US and international policy makers to address climate stabilization strategies; and advances effective distributed innovation theories, finance, and commercialization tools for new climate technologies.

International Renewable Energy Agency (IRENA)
PO Box 236
Masdar City, Abu Dhabi
United Arab Emirates
phone: +97124179000
email: info@irena.org
website: irena.org

The International Renewable Energy Agency (IRENA) is an intergovernmental organization that supports countries in their transition to a sustainable energy future. It serves as the principal platform for international cooperation, a center of excellence, and a repository of policy, technology, resource, and financial knowledge on renewable energy. IRENA promotes the widespread adoption and sustainable use of all forms of renewable energy, including bioenergy, geothermal, hydropower, ocean, solar, and wind energy in the pursuit of sustainable development, energy access, energy security, and low-carbon economic growth and prosperity.

Interstate Renewable Energy Council (IREC)
PO Box 1156
Latham, NY 12110-1156
phone: (518) 621-7379
email: info@irecusa.org
website: irecusa.org

The Interstate Renewable Energy Council (IREC) is an independent not-for-profit organization founded in 1982. It makes clean, efficient, sustainable energy possible for more Americans through forward-thinking regulatory reform, quality workforce development, and consumer education. Together, IREC's programs and initiatives empower consumers to make clean energy investments with confidence.

The Nature Conservancy

4245 N Fairfax Dr., Suite 100
Arlington, VA 22203-1606
phone: (703) 841-5300
email: magazine@tnc.org
website: www.nature.org

The mission of the Nature Conservancy is to conserve the lands and waters on which all life depends. Their vision is a world where the diversity of life thrives and people act to conserve nature for its own sake and its ability to fulfill our needs and enrich our lives. Through the dedication of more than 600 scientists and many partners—from individuals to governments to local nonprofits and corporations—the Nature Conservancy uses a collaborative approach to stay true to its core values.

Solar Energy Industries Association (SEIA)

600 14th St NW, Suite 400
Washington, DC 20005
phone: (202) 682-0556
email: info@seia.org
website: seia.org

The Solar Energy Industries Association (SEIA®) is the driving force behind solar energy and is building a strong solar industry to power America through advocacy and education. As the national trade association of the US solar energy industry, which now employs more than 250,000 Americans, they represent all organizations that promote, manufacture, install, and support the development of solar energy. SEIA works with its 1,000 member companies to build jobs and diversity, champion the use of cost-competitive solar in America, remove market barriers, and educate the public on the benefits of solar energy.

United States Energy Information Administration (EIA)
1000 Independence Ave. SW
Washington, DC 20585
phone: (202) 586-8800
email: infoctr@eia.gov
website: www.eia.gov

The US Energy Information Administration (EIA) collects, analyzes, and disseminates independent and impartial energy information to promote sound policymaking, efficient markets, and public understanding of energy and its interaction with the economy and the environment.

United States Renewable Energy Association (USREA)
PO Box 0550
Lexington, MI, 48450
phone: (810) 359-2250
email: support@usrea.org
website: usrea.org

The United States Renewable Energy Association (USREA) is a renewable energy advocacy group working to both educate and promote advanced technologies in the renewable energy industry. They provide a blog and news service online and encourage participation through knowledge posted by educational sources, corporate sources, and enthusiastic members alike.

Wind Energy Foundation (WEF)
1501 M St. SW
Washington, DC 20005
phone: (202) 580-6440
email: info@windenergyfoundation.org
website: windenergyfoundation.org

The Wind Energy Foundation (WEF) is a 501(c)(3) nonprofit organization dedicated to raising public awareness of wind as a clean, domestic energy source through communication, research, and education. WEF's campaigns and programs are aimed at educating decision makers, the media, and the general public about the economic and environmental benefits of wind energy and need for policy action to secure these benefits. They recruit, train, and mobilize leaders from the wind industry, other renewable energy sectors, and the broader community of supporters to deliver personalized messages about how renewable energy is helping to improve our economy and environment.

World Economic Forum
91-93 Route de la Capite
CH-1223 Cologny/Geneva
Switzerland
phone: +41 22 869 1212
email: contact@weforum.org
website: www.weforum.org

The World Economic Forum engages the foremost political, business, and other leaders of society to shape global, regional, and industry agendas. It was established in 1971 as a not-for-profit foundation and is headquartered in Geneva, Switzerland. It is independent, impartial, and not tied to any special interests. The Forum strives in all its efforts to demonstrate entrepreneurship in the global public interest while upholding the highest standards of governance.

World Energy Council
62-64 Cornhill
London EC3V 3NH
United Kingdom
phone: +44 (0) 207723 5996
website: www.worldenergy.org

The World Energy Council is a uniquely positioned organization that actively supports intergovernmental organizations, governments, and companies to deliver sustainable energy systems. The Council brings together all of the world's economic areas, every kind of energy ranging from renewables to fossil fuels, and every kind of organization.

Bibliography

Books

Olimpo Anaya-Lara, John Olav Tande, Kjetil Uhlen, and Karl Merz. *Offshore Wind Energy Technology*. Hoboken, NJ: Wiley, 2018.

Gretchen Bakke. *The Grid: The Fraying Wires Between Americans and Our Energy Future*. London, UK: Bloomsbury Publishing, 2016.

Godfrey Boyle. *Renewable Energy: Power for a Sustainable Future*. Oxford, UK: Oxford University Press, 2012.

David M. Buchla, Thomas E. Kissell, and Thomas L. Floyd. *Renewable Energy Systems*. New York, NY: Pearson, 2014.

Charles W Donovan. *Renewable Energy Finance: Powering the Future*. London, UK: Imperial College Press, 2015.

Martin Doyle. *The Source: How Rivers Made America and America Remade Its Rivers*. New York, NY: W. W. Norton & Company, 2018.

Oliver Haghi. *Alternative Energy: Oil and Gas*. New York, NY: Syrawood Publishing House, 2017.

Richard Heinberg and David Fridley. *Our Renewable Future: Laying the Path for One Hundred Percent Clean Energy*. Washington, DC: Island Press, 2016.

Sunggyu Lee and Y.T. Shah. *Biofuels and Bioenergy: Processes and Technologies* (Green Chemistry and Chemical Engineering). Boca Raton, FL: CRC Press, 2012.

Michael Peevey and Diane Wittenberg. *California Goes Green: A Roadmap to Climate Leadership*. Seattle, WA: Createspace Independent Publishing, 2017.

Richard Rhodes. *Energy: A Human History*. New York, NY: Simon & Schuster, 2018.

Tony Seba. *Clean Disruption of Energy and Transportation: How Silicon Valley Will Make Oil, Nuclear, Natural Gas, Coal, Electric Utilities, and Conventional Cars Obsolete by 2030*. Tony Seba, 2014.

Jeremy Shere. *Renewable: The World-Changing Power of Alternative Energy*. New York, NY: St. Martin's Press, 2013.

Varun Sivaram. *Taming the Sun: Innovations to Harness Solar Energy and Power the Planet*. Cambridge, MA: MIT Press, 2018.

Vaclav Smil. *Energy and Civilization: A History*. Cambridge, MA: MIT Press, 2017.

Michael E. Webber. *Thirst for Power: Energy, Water, and Human Survival*. New Haven, CT: Yale University Press, 2016.

Roland Wengenmayr, Thomas Bührke, and William D. Brewer. *Renewable Energy: Sustainable Energy Concepts for the Energy Change*. Weinheim, Germany: Wiley-VCH, 2012.

Periodicals and Internet Sources

Joanna Baker-Dowdell, "Cooperative Sees Farmers Generate and Trade Renewable Energy," *Advocate*, May 28, 2018. https://www.theadvocate.com.au/story/5434142/renewable-energy-co-op-launches-for-farmers/.

Michael J. Coren, "Companies Are Using California Homes as Batteries to Power the Grid," *Quartz*, May 25, 2018. https://qz.com/1288623/solar-energy-companies-are-using-california-homes-as-batteries-to-power-the-grid/.

Anmar Frangoul, "10 Massive Corporations Going Big on Solar Power," *CNBC.com*, May 27, 2018. https://www.cnbc.com/2018/05/28/10-massive-corporations-going-big-on-solar-power.html.

Steve Hanley, "DOE Research Grants Target Lower Cost Solar Power Grid Integration," *Clean Technica*, May 28, 2018. https://cleantechnica.com/2018/05/28/doe-research-grants-target-lower-cost-solar-power-grid-integration/.

Aloysius Low, "Fighting for Solar Power in a Concrete Jungle," *CNET*, May 24, 2018. https://www.cnet.com/news/fighting-for-solar-power-in-a-concrete-jungle/.

Tsvetana Paraskova, "IEA: Clean Energy Tech Falling Short of Climate Goals," *OilPrice.com*, May 23, 2018. https://oilprice.com/Latest-Energy-News/World-News/IEA-Clean-Energy-Tech-Falling-Short-Of-Climate-Goals.html.

Ivan Penn, "California Will Require Solar Power for New Homes," *New York Times*, May 9, 2018. https://www.nytimes.com/2018/05/09/business/energy-environment/california-solar-power.html.

Reason Staff, "Renewable Energy Mandates Are Making Poor People Poorer: New at Reason," *Reason.com*, May 28, 2018. https://reason.com/blog/2018/05/28/renewable-energy-mandates-are-making-poo.

Peter J. Reilly, "Where Will a Trillion Dollars in Clean Energy Investment Come From?" *Forbes*, May 28, 2018. https://www.forbes.com/sites/peterjreilly/2018/05/28/where-will-a-trillion-dollars-in-clean-energy-investment-come-from/#35954ac816de.

Isabelle Robinson, "Top 2018 Trends of Renewable Energy for Automotive Industry," *AZO Cleantech*, May 28, 2018. https://www.azocleantech.com/article.aspx?ArticleID=731.

Liji Thomas, "Creating Power from Rain Using Solar Panels," *AZO Cleantech*, May 16, 2018. https://www.azocleantech.com/article.aspx?ArticleID=725.

Mick Zawislak, "With Incentives, Solar Energy's Good for Environment, Business in Lake County," *Daily Herald*, May 27, 2018. http://www.dailyherald.com/business/20180527/with-incentives-solar-energys-good-for-environment-business-in-lake-county.

Index